4 ★ All-Star
Student Workbook

Linda Lee

Kristin Sherman ★ Grace Tanaka ★ Shirley Velasco

Second Edition

Connect
Learn
Succeed™

The McGraw·Hill Companies

Mc Graw Hill
Connect
Learn
Succeed™

ALL-STAR 4: WORKBOOK
Published by McGraw-Hill, a business unit of The McGraw-Hill Companies, Inc., 1221 Avenue of the Americas, New York, NY, 10020. Copyright © 2011 by The McGraw-Hill Companies, Inc. All rights reserved. Previous edition © 2005. No part of this publication may be reproduced or distributed in any form or by any means, or stored in a database or retrieval system, without the prior written consent of The McGraw-Hill Companies, Inc., including, but not limited to, in any network or other electronic storage or transmission, or broadcast for distance learning.

Some ancillaries, including electronic and print components, may not be available to customers outside the United States.

This book is printed on acid-free paper.

1 2 3 4 5 6 7 8 9 0 WDQ/WDQ 1 0 9 8 7 6 5 4 3 2 1 0

Workbook

ISBN 978-0-07-719727-8
MHID 0-07-719727-5

ISE

ISBN 978-0-07-131389-6
MHID 0-07-131389-3

Vice president/Editor in chief: *Elizabeth Haefele*
Vice president/Director of marketing: *John E. Biernat*
Director of development, ESL Domestic: *Valerie E. Kelemen*
Developmental editor: *Laura LeDrean*
Director of sales and marketing, ESL Domestic: *Pierre Montagano*
Lead digital product manager: *Damian Moshak*
Digital developmental editor: *Kevin White*
Director, Editing/Design/Production: *Jess Ann Kosic*
Project manager: *Jean R. Starr*
Senior production supervisor: *Debra R. Sylvester*
Senior designer: *Srdjan Savanovic*
Senior photo research coordinator: *Lori Kramer*
Photo researcher: *Allison Grimes*
Digital production coordinator: *Brent dela Cruz*
Typeface: *11/13 Frutiger Roman*
Compositor: *Laserwords Private Limited*
Printer: *World Color Press Inc.*
Cover credit: *Andrew Lange*
Credits: The credits section for this book begins on page 187 and is considered an extension of the copyright page.

The Internet addresses listed in the text were accurate at the time of publication. The inclusion of a Web site does not indicate an endorsement by the authors or McGraw-Hill, and McGraw-Hill does not guarantee the accuracy of the information presented at these sites.

www.mhhe.com

All-Star is a four-level, standards-based series for English learners featuring a picture-dictionary approach to vocabulary building. "Big picture" scenes in each unit provide springboards to a wealth of activities developing all of the language skills. Each *All-Star* Workbook unit provides 18 pages of supplementary activities for its corresponding Student Book unit. The workbook activities offer students further practice in developing the language, vocabulary, and life-skill competencies taught in the Student Book. Answers to the Workbook activities are available in the Teacher's Edition.

Workbook Features

★ **Standards coverage complements the Student Book** for a comprehensive program covering all revised national standards: CASAS, SCANS, EFF, Florida, LAUSD, Texas, and others.

★ **Wide range of exercises** can be used by students working independently or in groups, in the classroom, with a tutor, or at home. Each unit includes several activities that allow students to interact, usually by asking and answering questions.

★ **Alternate application lessons** complement the Student Book application lesson, inviting students to tackle work, family, and/or community extension activities in each unit.

★ **Student Book page references** at the top of each Workbook page show how the two components support one another.

★ **Practice tests** at the end of each unit provide practice answering multiple-choice questions such as those found on the CASAS tests. Students are invited to chart their progress on these tests on a bar graph on the inside back cover.

★ **Crossword puzzles and word searches** reinforce unit vocabulary.

Alternate Application Lessons (Work, Family, Community)

Equipped for the Future (EFF) is a set of standards for adult literacy and lifelong learning developed by The National Institute for Literacy (www.nifl.gov). The organizing principle of EFF is that adults assume responsibilities in three major areas of life—as workers, as parents, and as citizens. These three areas of focus are called "role maps" in the EFF documentation.

Lesson 4 in each unit of the Student Book provides a real-life application relating to one of the learners' roles. The Workbook includes two alternate application lessons that expand on two of the three roles. This allows you, as the teacher, to customize the unit to meet the needs of your students. You can teach any or all of the application lessons in class. For example, if all your students work, you may choose to focus on the work applications. If your students have diverse interests and needs, you may have them work in small groups on different applications. If your program provides many hours of classroom time each week, you have the material to cover all three roles.

Contents

Have We Met Before?

A **Conversation Challenge**. Practice the conversation with a partner. Then practice the conversation again. Replace the underlined words with your own ideas.

A: Hi. My name's <u>Carlos</u>.

B: Hi, <u>Carlos</u>. I'm <u>Linda</u>. It's nice to meet you.

A: Nice to meet you, too. When did you move here?

B: I moved here <u>five years ago</u>.

A: Did you come here with your family?

B: <u>Yes, I moved here with my husband and son.</u> <u>My son is 12.</u> How about you?

A: <u>I moved here in 2010 with my parents and my brother.</u>

B: Where are you from?

A: I am from <u>São Paulo</u>.

B: How interesting. What is it like there?

A: <u>It's the largest city in South America. It is very cosmopolitan. It's a lot like Los Angeles.</u> What about you?

B: <u>I am from a small village in Mexico. It's not like Los Angeles at all. Life is very quiet there.</u>

B Complete the chart below with information about some of your family members. Then describe your family members to a partner.

NAME	RELATION	DESCRIPTION	
		(age, height, hair color, etc.)	(personality)
Paul	father	71 years old, 5 feet 6 inches tall, brown hair, brown eyes	funny, likes to tell jokes

C Look at the categories below. How is your culture similar to or different from U.S. culture? Make notes in the chart. Then discuss your answers with a partner.

CELEBRATIONS AND HOLIDAYS	FAMILIES	MAKING FRIENDS	PARTIES	SCHOOL	WORK

D Conversation Challenge. Practice the conversation with a partner. Then practice the conversation again. Replace the underlined words with your own ideas.

A: Do you have a job?

B: Yes, I do. I work in a lawyer's office. I'm a receptionist. I started that job in 2011.

A: Oh, that sounds interesting.* What do you do for that job?

B: I answer phones and take messages. I also greet clients and keep an appointment book.

A: What other kinds of jobs have you had?

B: I was a stockperson in a grocery store from 2007 to 2010. I was responsible for stocking the meat and dairy items. I also had to order food and clean the stockroom once a week. And after that, I was a salesclerk in a clothing store for two years. I helped customers, folded clothes, and used the cash register. How about you?

---

*Useful Expressions

to show interest

Oh, that sounds interesting.
Really?
Are you? / Were you? / Do you?

Exploring Continuing Education

A Unscramble the questions. Then use the course schedule to answer the questions.

1. does / meet / the keyboarding class / when

   When does the keyboarding class meet?

   It meets from 7 to 8.

2. the computer repair class / when / begin / does

   _____?

   _____.

3. which course / the cheapest / is

   _____?

   _____.

4. the most expensive / are / which two courses

   _____?

   _____.

5. the writing course / weeks / does / how many / last

   _____?

   _____.

6. how much / to take / writing II / would it cost / and keyboarding

   _____?

   _____.

7. do students / in which courses / probably use computers

   _____?

   _____.

8. improve your health / might help you / which courses

   _____?

   _____.

SANTA MONICA Continuing Education Course Schedule Wednesday Evening Classes				
COURSE	**WKS.**	**TIME**	**TUITION**	
Auto Body Repair	12	6:30–9:30	$145	B3
Basic Computer Skills	10	7:00–9:00	$124	B307
Careers in Banking	8	6:30–9:00	$109	B223
Computer Repair	10	6:30–9:30	$149	B234
Defensive Driving	1	7:45–10:00	$45	PE22
Drawing Workshop	8	6:30–9:00	$124	W453
Interviewing Skills	12	6:00–9:00	$165	Th43
Italian Cooking	10	7:00–8:30	$89	B304
Keyboarding	8	7:00–8:00	$120	B231
Photography	8	6:45–9:45	$149	B303
Pottery I	10	6:00–8:30	$109	B308
Public Speaking	8	7:00–9:00	$109	B302
Small Engine Repair	12	7:00–9:00	$165	B306
Stress Management	12	4:00–5:00	$89	W233
Tai Chi	10	7:00–8:30	$75	B305
Writing II	10	7:00–9:00	$124	B301

B In which classes might you hear someone say the things below?

1. Are there any more aprons? _(mandil)_ _____ _Italian cooking and pottery_ _____

2. Which button should I push? _____

3. Did you turn the oven on? _____

4. Could you please turn the light off? _____

5. How does it taste? _____

6. Relax and take a deep breath. _____

C Choose an adjective to complete each sentence below. (More than one answer is possible.)

interesting	important	helpful
boring	unimportant	unhelpful
useful	common	necessary
useless	unusual	unnecessary

1. Knowing how to cook is a very _____ skill.

2. It's _____ to learn how to make pottery.

3. Knowing how to speak in public is _____ for supervisors.

4. Knowing how to use a computer is _____ for teachers.

5. It's _____ for everyone to know how to manage stress.

6. It's _____ to know how to use a keyboard if you want to use a computer.

7. Knowing how to repair engines is very _____.

8. It's _____ to improve your interviewing skills before you go for a job interview.

9. I think it would be _____ to work in a bank.

10. It's _____ for children to study a foreign language.

D Choose a profession and a skill to complete each question below. Then circle your answer.

Professions				**Skills**	
teacher	mechanic	photographer		drive a car	speak a foreign language
doctor	waiter	file clerk		add and subtract	give clear instructions
farmer	tailor	reporter		repair equipment	read

1. Do you think a _____ needs to know how to _____? YES NO

2. Does a _____ need to know how to _____? YES NO

3. Do you think a _____ needs to know how to _____? YES NO

4. Does a _____ need to know how to _____? YES NO

5

Identifying Interpersonal Skills

A Add the missing words to the chart and complete the questions below. Then answer the questions.

ADJECTIVES	ADVERBS
1.	essentially
2. clear	
3. concise	
4.	proficiently
5.	responsibly
6.	cooperatively
7. different	
8. good	
9.	possibly
10.	easily

1. What is _____essential_____ for all children to have? _____

2. Was the sky _____ yesterday? _____

3. Is it important to give instructions _____ in an emergency? _____

4. How long does it take to become a _____ driver? _____

5. Who is _____ for cooking in your family? _____

6. Why is it sometimes difficult to work _____? _____

7. How is English _____ from your first language? _____

8. What do you wish you could do _____? _____

9. Is it _____ for an immigrant to become a U.S. senator or representative? _____

10. What sport is _____ to learn how to play? _____

B Match the words that are similar in meaning. Write the words on the lines.

h 1. necessary _____essential_____   a. concentrate

i 2. act _____   b. come up with

e 3. skillful _____   c. concise

a 4. focus _____   d. improve

f 5. understand _____   e. proficient

g 6. answer _____   f. comprehend

c 7. brief _____   g. respond

b 8. think of _____   h. essential

d 9. get better _____   i. behave

C Complete the sentences with words from the box.

> distracted   behavior   affect   left out
> share   resolved   interact   interpersonal
> proficient   come up with

1. Five people live in my apartment; each person pays an equal_____ of the rent.

2. The cake tasted very strange because the chef_____ the eggs.

3. The noise of the children _____ me from my work.

4. What are the rules of _____ in the library?

5. Most people look down at the floor when they are riding in an elevator; they don't _____ with the other people in the elevator.

6. A _____ public speaker can speak clearly and concisely.

7. Jim and Bob weren't able to work together until they _____ their differences.

8. Eating less food should _____ your weight.

9. People with poor _____ skills have trouble getting along with others.

10. It took us several weeks to _____ a name for our restaurant.

D Complete the sentences. Use the simple past or the present perfect form of the verb in parentheses.

1. Peter _____*has been*_____ (be) a cook for five years.

2. At the end of last year, he _____ (decide) he wanted a change.

3. In January, he _____ (register) for classes at the community college.

4. So far, he _____ (take) two accounting classes and one computer class.

5. He is happy because he _____ (learn) a lot in the past six months.

6. The classes _____ (teach) him how to keep accounts.

7. He _____ (improve / also) his computer skills.

7. Last month, he _____ (create) his own spreadsheet and _____ (write) a business plan.

8. He _____ (meet / also) some interesting people at the college.

9. One of his new friends _____ (help) him write a resume last week.

10. The classes and his classmates _____ (make) Peter more confident to make a career change.

Taking Telephone Messages

A Number each conversation in order starting with #1.

Conversation A

_____ Thank you.

_____ You're welcome.

_____ Yes, that's right.

_____ That was ten o'clock?

___1___ Henry's Market. How can I help you?

_____ We're open until ten tonight.

_____ I'm just calling to find out when you close tonight.

Conversation B

_____ Okay. I'll give him the message.

_____ I'm sorry, but he's not here right now. Can I take a message?

_____ Do you want me to have him call you back?

___1___ Hello.

_____ Sure. Could you just tell him that Jeff called?

_____ Yes, if he could call me back tonight that would be great.

_____ Anytime before 9 would be fine.

_____ Hi. Is Arun there?

_____ How late can he call?

_____ Great. Thanks.

Conversation C

_____ Can you tell her I called?

_____ Yes. This is Rebecca West. I'm returning Dr. Sayers' call.

_____ Yes, of course. Your name again, please?

___1___ Dr. Sayers' office. Can I help you?

_____ And your telephone number?

_____ I'm sorry, but Dr. Sayers just left the office.

_____ It's 555-2345. And tell her I'll be at home this evening.

_____ Thank you.

_____ It's Dr. Rebecca West.

_____ I'll give her the message, Dr. West.

Conversation D

_____ Okay. I'll tell her you called.

_____ I'm sorry, but she's not here right now. Can I take a message?

_____ Yes, it's A-b-r-a-m-s. And my number is 555-3994.

_____ Yes, could you tell her Barbara Abrams from Easy Construction called?

_____ Could you spell your last name for me please?

_____ Hi. I'd like to speak to Maria Azula, please.

_____ Thank you very much.

_____ You're welcome.

___1___ Metro Supply. This is Joe speaking.

8

later ✓

B Use Conversations C and D on page 8 to complete the telephone messages.

C

WHILE YOU WERE OUT

FOR: _____
DATE: 1/23   TIME: 10:30 a.m.
FROM: _____
OF: _____
PHONE: _____
EMAIL: _____

☐ Telephoned   ☐ Will Call Again
☐ Returned Call   ☐ Please See Me
☐ Please Call   ☐ Important

MESSAGE: _____
_____
_____

D

WHILE YOU WERE OUT

FOR: _____
DATE: 2/18   TIME: 10:30 a.m.
FROM: _____
OF: _____
PHONE: _____
EMAIL: _____

☐ Telephoned   ☐ Will Call Again
☐ Returned Call   ☐ Please See Me
☐ Please Call   ☐ Important

MESSAGE: _____
_____
_____

C Complete the sentences with *should* or *shouldn't*.

1. You _____ speak clearly when you talk on the telephone.
2. You _____ use words such as "you guys" on the telephone at work.
3. You _____ talk on your cell phone in a restaurant.
4. You _____ leave long messages on a telephone answering machine.
5. You _____ speak softly on a cell phone when you are on a bus or train.
6. You _____ identify yourself when you leave a message on an answering machine.
7. You _____ put someone on hold for a long time.
8. You _____ always say "Goodbye" before you hang up the phone.

D Complete the answering machine messages with your own ideas.

1.
"Hi _____. This is your employee _____. I'm calling to _____
_____.
Please call me back when you have a chance. My number is _____. Thank you. Bye."

2.
"Hi _____. This is _____. I'm calling to _____
_____
_____
Thanks. Bye."

9

Setting Goals for Learning New Skills

A Add the missing job title to each job description. Write the job titles on the lines.

JOB TITLES

Childcare Worker
Computer Programmer
Office Manager

Line Cook
Real Estate Agent
Medical Assistant

Job Title: _Childcare Worker_

Job Description:

Available position in our toddler room. Teacher will be responsible for ten 3- to 4-year-olds. Five years experience working in a school setting, excellent interpersonal skills required. Bilingual Cantonese/English a plus.

Education: Certificate in Child Development

Job Classification: Full Time

Job Benefits:

Health Insurance   Paid Vacation

Job Title: _OFFICE Mgr._

Job Description:

The person in this position will be responsible for payroll and taxes and general office duties in a family law office. Candidates should have strong communication and PC skills.

Education: Certificate in Accounting required.

Job Classification: Full Time

Job Benefits:

Health Insurance   Dental Insurance
401K   Paid Vacation

Job Title: _Computer Programmer_

Job Description:

Downtown medical clinic is now hiring. Job includes technical support for entire office. Potential candidates should have excellent team skills.

Education: Bachelor's Degree in Computer Science

Job Classification: Full Time

Job Benefits:

Health Insurance   Telecommuting
401K   Paid Vacation

Job Title: _Line Cook_

Job Description:

This cooking position requires good communication and team skills. Hotel cooking experience and a culinary degree preferred. Knowledge of cooking, ingredients, and procedures preferred. Bilingual Spanish and English. Hours are 6 AM to 2 PM.

Education: High School Degree or GED

Job Classification: Full Time

Job Benefits:

Health Insurance   Uniform Allowance

Job Title: _Real Estate Agent_

Job Description:

Fast-paced friendly office is seeking an energetic person who likes to work with people. The candidate should have excellent interpersonal skills and experience in sales. Valid California Real Estate license, driver's license, and car required.

Education: Real Estate Certificate

Job Classification: Full Time

Job Benefits:

Flexible Schedule   Annual Bonus

Job Title: _____

Job Description:

The person in this position will assist doctors and nurses in the Emergency Room. Hours are midnight to 8:00 A.M. Fluency in several languages a plus.

Education: Bachelor's Degree and Nursing or Medical Assistant Certificate

Job Classification: Full Time

Job Benefits:

Health Insurance   Dental Insurance
Uniform Allowance   Paid Vacation

B Read the description of each person. Find the best match for a job from Activity A for each person. Write the job title next to the person.

Job	Descriptions
_____ _____	1. **Marta** wants to work in an office. She likes to work with numbers, and she has strong computer skills. She wants a job that offers a 401K plan and health insurance. She is shy and has trouble talking to people. She has a Bachelor's degree in Computer Science. She speaks English and Spanish fluently.
_____ _____	2. **Tina** is looking for a job working with computers. She likes working with a lot of people and is a great team member. She has a Certificate in Computer Programming. The most important job benefit for her is the ability to telecommute. She speaks some Cantonese.
_____ _____	3. **Alex** wants to work in the medical field. He likes working with people. He has a Bachelor's Degree in Biology. He is taking his first Spanish class this semester. He speaks English fluently.
_____ _____	4. **Cara** is an excellent salesperson. She sold cars for ten years, and her customers always enjoyed working with her. Last year, she sold more cars than anyone else at her company, and she received a new car as a bonus. She has a Bachelor's Degree.
_____ _____	5. **Ed** likes working with children. He was a kindergarten teacher for eight years before his children were born. He stayed home with his children until they started school. Now he wants to go back to work. He has a Master's Degree in Education.
_____ _____	6. **Luis** is fluent in Spanish and he can communicate in English. He likes to cook and he enjoys working with other people. He graduated from high school a year ago. Next year, he plans to enroll in a program to become a paralegal, but this year he needs to make some money. He has never worked before.

C Complete the chart below with information from Activities A and B.

Person / Job	What skills and education does the person need to get?	What should the person do?
Marta / _____		
Tina / _____		
Alex / _____		
Cara / _____		
Ed / _____		
Luis / _____		

Unit 1: Skills and Abilities

Reading: Making Inferences

A What can you infer from each sentence below? Check (✓) the logical inferences.

1. My friend Ted always does his share of the work.

   ☐ Ted is friendly.   ☐ Ted isn't lazy.   ☐ Ted is the hardest worker.

2. Julia never makes any spelling or grammar mistakes when she writes in English.

   ☐ Julia speaks only English.   ☐ Julia is an accurate writer.   ☐ Julia loves to write.

3. Daniela got a promotion even though she has only worked there for a year.

   ☐ Daniela is a good employee.   ☐ Daniela asked for a promotion.   ☐ Daniela plans to quit soon.

4. When Manuel was sick, a lot of people came to visit him.

   ☐ Manuel took a lot of sick days.   ☐ Manuel has a lot of friends.   ☐ Manuel was sick for a long time.

5. Paul didn't answer a lot of the questions on the test because he couldn't concentrate.

   ☐ Paul is a difficult student.   ☐ Paul didn't want to take the test.   ☐ Paul didn't do well on the test.

6. Akiko always speaks softly when she talks on her cell phone in public places.

   ☐ Akiko is polite.   ☐ Akiko doesn't like to talk on the phone.   ☐ Akiko has a cheap phone.

B Based on the facts in each statement, write an inference.

1. John always wears a suit and tie to work.

   _____

2. Amelia always sits alone in the cafeteria.

   _____

3. Sam always gets to work early.

   _____

4. Pam's desk is messy.

   _____

5. Marco never does his homework, and neither does Sue.

   _____

C Read the article and answer the questions below.

#HW
for
4/5

Talent in Two Languages Can Boost Your Career Value

by Deborah Willoughby

When Spanish-speaking people come into the Probate Office of Montgomery County, Alabama, to renew their car tags[1], many ask for Christie Vazquez.

"They feel more comfortable with people who speak their language," said Vazquez, a clerk who is fluent in Spanish. Vazquez often is called on to help communicate with Spanish-speaking customers throughout the probate department.

As the country becomes more diverse[2], businesses are responding to a greater number of people, both employees and customers, who don't speak English. Learning another language may not be the easiest career-development move[3], but it may be among the most useful.

"Folks who are bilingual are going to be much more employable than those who speak just one language," said Walt Hines, who teaches introductory Spanish at a Montgomery technical college.

[1] tags: car license plates
[2] diverse: varied
[3] career-development move: thing you can do to build your career

---

1. What skill does Christie Vazquez have that her coworkers don't have?

   _____

2. Why is there a growing need for employees who speak two languages?

   _____

3. Why is learning another language a useful career-development move?

   _____

4. What is Walt Hines's profession?

   _____

5. What can you infer from the information in the article? Check (✓) your answers.

   ☐ Christie Vazquez grew up in Mexico.

   ☐ Christie Vazquez has worked at the probate office for many years.

   ☐ A number of Spanish-speaking people live in Montgomery County, Alabama.

   ☐ Vazquez is bilingual.

   ☐ Walt Hines in a native Spanish speaker.

   ☐ Walt Hines speaks some Spanish.

Writing: Business Letters

A Choose the correct words to complete the descriptions of the parts of a business letter.

heading	salutation	body
inside address	signature	closing

1. The word "Sincerely" is a common _____ for a business letter.

2. The sender's address is included in the _____.

3. You should handwrite your _____ rather than typing or printing it.

4. The _____ of a letter is the main part.

5. The date is part of the _____.

6. The receiver's address is in the _____.

7. "Dear Sir / Madam" is an example of a _____.

B Use the information on the envelope to complete the letter below.

Ray Jones
245 Harvey Street
Pacoima, CA 91331

Mr. Ian Talbot, Manager
Lexon Real Estate
7676 Jackson Street
Reseda, CA 91335

_____

_____

_____

_____

_____

_____

_____

February 18, 2011

Dear Mr. Talbot,

I was excited to read about the job opening for
an Administrative Assistant at Lexon Real Estate. I
have several years of experience in a variety of fields
including real estate.

C Add a date, a salutation, and a closing to the letter below.

HW
4/19

44 Highland Avenue
Gardena, CA 90248

_____

Ms. Vera Lane
Manager Computer Giant
432 Winston Avenue
North Hollywood, CA 91001

_____

    Thank you for taking the time to meet with me yesterday to discuss the position of Sales Supervisor at Computer Giant. I sincerely enjoyed meeting with you and learning more about the company.

    Our conversation made me even more interested in becoming part of Computer Giant's sales team. Computer Giant is an exciting company with a quality product and excellent customer service. I am confident that my experience and my leadership skills would make me a strong Sales Supervisor.

    Please feel free to contact me if I can provide you with any further information. I look forward eagerly to hearing from you, and thank you again for your time.

_____

Robert Hunter
Robert Hunter

D Answer the questions about the business letter in Activity C.

1. Who is the writer of the letter?

_____

2. What is his address?

_____

3. What is the purpose of the letter?

_____

4. Why does the writer think he is qualified for the job?

_____

5. Do you think this letter is clear or not clear? Why?

_____

Family: Parents and Teachers

A For each category below, add 2 more examples.

Category	Examples
1) Ways parents can be involved in their children's education	• they can volunteer at school • •
2) Ways parents can discipline their children	• they can take something away • •
3) Way parents can encourage their children to read	• they can praise them • •

B Read the article below. How important do you think it is for parents to do each thing? Write *VI (very important), SI (somewhat important),* or *NI (not important)* on the lines.

Eight Things Teachers Wish Parents Would Do
Brought to you by the National PTA®

1. **Be involved**. Parent involvement helps students learn, improves schools, and helps teachers work with you to help your children succeed. _____

2. **Provide resources at home for learning.** Use your local library, and have books and magazines available in your home. Read with your children each day. _____

3. **Set a good example.** Show your children by your own actions that you believe reading is both enjoyable and useful. Monitor[1] television viewing. _____

4. **Encourage students to do their best in school.** Show your children that you believe education is important and that you want them to do their best. _____

5. **Value education and seek a balance[2] between schoolwork and outside activities.** Emphasize[3] your children's progress in developing the knowledge and skills they need to be successful both in school and in life. _____

6. **Support school rules and goals.** Take care not to undermine[4] school rules, discipline, or goals. _____

7. **Use pressure[5] positively.** Encourage children to do their best, but don't pressure them by setting goals too high or by scheduling too many activities. _____

8. **Call teachers early if you think there's a problem.** Call while there is still time to solve the problem. Don't wait for teachers to call you. _____

[1]monitor: observe, watch over
[2]balance: not too much of one or the other
[3]emphasize: place importance on

[4]undermine: ruin the efforts of
[5]pressure: the making of demands

Excerpted with permission from National PTA®, "Ten Things Teachers Wish Parents Would Do." For additional parent involvement resources, visit PTA.org.

C Which of the suggestions from Activity B are these parents following? Write your answers.

HW
4/19
24

1. Sonya reads to her children before they go to bed every night.
   She provides resources at home for learning.

2. When Tomi's children were young, she almost never watched TV.

   _____

3. Regina and Paolo praise their daughter a lot when she gets good grades.

   _____

4 Marie volunteers at her children's school three hours a week. She usually helps out in the library.

   _____

5. Ali's son suddenly stopped doing his homework at school. Ali called his son's teachers right away to find out if something had happened at school.

   _____

D Choose the correct form of the words to complete the questions. Then ask a classmate.

NOUN	VERB	ADJECTIVE
1. involvement	involve	XXXXX
2. success	succeed	successful
3. action	act	active
4. enjoyment	enjoy	enjoyable
5. encouragement	encourage	XXXXX
6. education	educate	educational
7. support	support	supportive
8. discipline	discipline	disciplinary

1. What _____ should grandparents have in their grandchildren's education?
2. What is the secret to being a _____ parent?
3. Why are some children more _____ than others?
4 Do you think going to the library is _____?
5. How can you _____ children to do their homework?
6. How important is it to get a good _____?
7. Who gave you a lot of _____ when you were a child?
8. In the U.S., what are unacceptable ways to _____ a child?

Community: At School

A Complete the instructions below with the words from the box

due for 4/24

attending	immunization	enroll	register
proof	required	determine	

BEFORE YOUR CHILD STARTS SCHOOL

If you would like to _____ your child in school in the Los Angeles Unified School District, please follow these steps.

1. _____ your child's school of residence. Go to www.lausd.net and click on "Parents/Guardians." Under "Resources," click on "School Finder." Enter your address and click "Submit." You will see a list of the schools in your neighborhood.

2. _____ your child at his or her school of residence. Bring _____ of your child's age (birth certificate, baptismal certificate, passport, etc.) and proof of residence (such as a utility bill). You must also bring proof of your child's shots. Bring health and _____ records signed by a public health clinic, health care provider, or private doctor. Your child must have all of the _____ shots before _____ school. For information about the shots your child needs, call the LAUSD's School Nursing Services.

B Answer the questions with information from Activity A.

1. Which website should you visit to find your child's school of residence?

_____

_____

2. What are two things you need to bring when you register your child for school?

_____

_____

3. When must your child have his or her shots?

_____

_____

4. Whom should you call to ask what shots your child needs?

_____

_____

C Read the note below. Underline the length of time and the reason Elena is going to miss school. On a separate piece of paper, write a note using the cues in the box.

Dear Mr. Jones,

Please excuse my daughter Elena from school for the next four days. She has the flu, and the doctor wants her to stay home for the rest of the week.

My son will come to your class at the end of each day to pick up Elena's homework assignments.

Sincerely,

Teresa Salas

Hw) for 4/24

Parent: Lisa Chen
Teacher: Ms. Myers
Student: Judy Chen
Length of time: three days
Reason: Her grandfather died. She has to go out of town for the funeral.
Extra information: Judy's friend Kelli will pick up homework assignments.

D **Conversation Challenge.** Read the conversation with a partner.

A: Administration Office. This is Ms. Van. How can I help you?

B: Hello, Ms. Van. This is Tommy Kim's mother, Mrs. Kim. I'm calling because <u>my son has to leave early today. He has a dentist's appointment.</u>

A: OK. <u>What time does he have to leave today</u>?

B: He <u>has to leave at 1:30.</u>

A: All right. You'll need to come into the office and fill out an early dismissal form.

B: OK. I'll do that when I pick him up. Thanks, Ms. Van.

Now practice the conversation again. Replace the underlined words with the ideas in the box or your own ideas.

Tommy is going to be late.	Tommy has to leave early.	Tommy will not be in school today.
He missed the school bus.	He has a doctor's appointment.	He's not feeling well.
He'll be at school at 8:30.	He has to leave at noon.	He'll be back in school on Monday.
Write a note.	Come to the office to sign him out.	Send a doctor's note.

Practice Test

DIRECTIONS: Read the business letter below to answer the next 4 questions. Use the Answer Sheet.

122 Fifth St., Apt. 5B
Pomona, CA 91730

January 10, 2011

Product Safety Department

Just 4 Fun Toys

19850 Temple Road

Gardena, CA 90248

To Whom It May Concern:

   On December 23rd, I purchased a Rolling Rover toy at your store in San José, California. Soon after I gave it to my two-year-old son, one of the small wheels came off. Since these wheels are small enough for a child to swallow, I am very concerned that this toy could cause injury to another child.

   I urge you to correct this problem quickly so that no children are harmed in the future.

Yours truly,

Geneva Spring

Geneva Spring

ANSWER SHEET

1	Ⓐ	Ⓑ	Ⓒ	Ⓓ
2	Ⓐ	Ⓑ	Ⓒ	Ⓓ
3	Ⓐ	Ⓑ	Ⓒ	Ⓓ
4	Ⓐ	Ⓑ	Ⓒ	Ⓓ
5	Ⓐ	Ⓑ	Ⓒ	Ⓓ
6	Ⓐ	Ⓑ	Ⓒ	Ⓓ
7	Ⓐ	Ⓑ	Ⓒ	Ⓓ
8	Ⓐ	Ⓑ	Ⓒ	Ⓓ
9	Ⓐ	Ⓑ	Ⓒ	Ⓓ
10	Ⓐ	Ⓑ	Ⓒ	Ⓓ

1. What was the writer's purpose for writing this letter?
   A. to thank someone for something
   B. to ask a question
   C. to ask for money
   D. to report a problem

2. Where is the writer's address?
   A. on the upper right side
   B. on the upper left side
   C. on the lower left side
   D. on the lower right side

3. What other salutation could you use for a business letter?
   A. Yours truly,
   B. Hi
   C. Dear Sir / Madam:
   D. Your friend,

4. Where did the writer sign the letter?
   A. below the heading
   B. above the closing
   C. below the closing
   D. above the salutation

DIRECTIONS: Read the job interview tips to answer the next 6 questions. Use the Answer Sheet on page 20.

HW for 4/20

JOB INTERVIEW TIPS

1) Leave extra time to get to a job interview. It's important that you arrive a few minutes before the interview is supposed to begin.

2) Make sure your appearance is neat and dress appropriately. It's usually better to be overdressed than underdressed.

3) Try not to appear nervous during the interview. Avoid nervous habits such as chewing gum and playing with things in your hand.

4) Speak clearly and concisely and always tell the truth.

5) Make eye contact with the interviewer and speak confidently.

6) Focus on what you can do for the company. Wait until you have been offered the job to ask about the salary and benefits.

7) Use examples from your work and educational background to show that you are hard working, honest, responsible, and a team player.

8) At the end of the interview, shake hands and thank the interviewer for his or her time. You can also say that you are looking forward to hearing from him or her.

5. According to the article, when should you arrive at a job interview?

A. exactly on time

B. a half hour early

C. a little early

D. a little late

6. According to the article, what is one sign of nervousness?

A. looking around

B. playing with things in your hand

C. making eye contact

D. arriving early

7. Which example would show you are a hard worker?

A. I grew up on a farm.

B. I like to get up early in the morning.

C. In addition to my job, I am taking two evening courses.

D. I think I'm a hard worker.

8. Which of these things shouldn't you do at a job interview?

A. speak clearly

B. look directly at the interviewer

C. ask first about the job benefits

D. dress neatly

9. What could you say to show that you are a team player?

A. I enjoy working on group projects.

B. I have a big family.

C. I like team sports.

D. I like to meet new people.

10. Which sentence would be appropriate for you to say at the end of a job interview?

A. When will I hear from you?

B. I hope you don't interview anyone else.

C. I'll call you tomorrow.

D. Thank you for your time.

HOW DID YOU DO? Count the number of correct answers on your answer sheet. Record this number in the bar graph on the inside back cover.

Describing Transportation Problems

A Write the correct transportation problem under each picture.

> car trouble   flat tire   car accident   stuck in traffic

1

Andy

_____

2

Carla

_____

3

_____

4

Tom

_____

B Write sentences about the people and transportation problems in Activity A.

1. _____

2. _____

3. _____

4. _____

C Number the sentences in the correct order.

_____7_____ Finally, I saw my exit and got off the highway.

_____5_____ The other driver and I stopped and exchanged insurance information. Fortunately, no one was hurt.

_____2_____ The traffic was worse than usual because a car with a flat tire was stopped in the middle of the highway.

_____3_____ I was right behind the car with the flat tire, so I tried to change lanes.

_____10_____ The officer was very friendly, but he still gave me a ticket.

_____8_____ When I got off the highway, I drove fast to get to my son's school on time. I had to pick him up before 6:00 PM, so I was going 35 miles per hour in a 25-mile zone.

_____4_____ When I started to change lanes, I hit the car next to me.

_____9_____ A police officer pulled me over when I was just one block from the school.

_____1_____ I was driving home from work on Friday when I got stuck in rush hour traffic.

_____6_____ Then I got back in my car and drove on the highway for another half an hour.

D Answer the questions with complete sentences.

1. Have you ever been in a car accident or seen a car accident? If yes, describe what happened.

   _____

   _____

   _____

2. Has a family member or friend ever been in a car accident? If yes, describe what happened.

   _____

   _____

   _____

3. Has a police officer ever stopped you for speeding? How about a family member or friend? If yes, describe what happened.

   _____

   _____

   _____

4. Have you ever had a flat tire? How about a family member or friend? If yes, describe what happened.

   _____

   _____

   _____

Understanding Insurance Terms

A Match the words that are similar in meaning. Write the words on the lines.

1. incredibly ___g___
2. cover ___a___
3. collide ___i___
4. deduct ___b___
5. amount ___h___
6. cost ___d___
7. request ___c___
8. essential ___e___
9. accurate ___f___

a. include
b. subtract
c. ask for
d. price
e. necessary
f. correct
g. very; extremely
h. quantity
i. hit

B Add the missing noun and verb forms to the chart. Use the correct form of each word in the questions below. Then answer the questions.

NOUNS	VERBS
1. *collision*	collide
2. payment	pay
3. insurance	insure
4. agreement	agree
5. coverage	cover
6. injury	injure

1. What might cause two cars to _____?

_____

2. What monthly _____ do you make?

_____

3. Do you have health _____?

_____

4. What are you and your friends usually in _____ about?

_____

_____

5. Does your insurance _____ your personal possessions?

_____

6. What can people do to reduce their chance of _____ in a car accident?

_____

C Add the missing words to the sentences below.

claim	comprehensive	medical	policy
collision	bodily injury	uninsured motorist	premium

1. The _____ is the amount of money you pay for your insurance.

2. The contract between the driver and the insurance company is called a _____.

3. If you hit a wall or some other object, your _____ coverage will pay for the damage to your car.

4. If your car is stolen, your _____ coverage will pay for the loss.

5. It's important to have _____ insurance if you injure someone else in a car accident.

6. _____ insurance helps to pay medical expenses for the driver of the policy holder's car and any passengers.

7. If you want to collect insurance money after an accident, you have to file a _____.

8. If your car is hit by someone without car insurance, _____ insurance will help to pay for injuries to the people in your car.

D Complete the paragraph with the correct article: *a/an*, *the* or Ø.

Sam had ___a___(1) bad day today. He did not hear ___the___(2) alarm this morning and woke up

late. It was ___a___(3) cold day, and ___the___(4) streets were icy. Sam was in ___a___(5) hurry,

so he didn't eat ___Ø___(6) breakfast. On his way to work, Sam lost control of his car and hit

___a___(7) tree. Sam was not hurt, but ___the___(8) front end of ___the___(9) car was dam-

aged. He decided he should not drive ___the___(10) car. Instead he called ___a___(11) tow truck to

take him to ___a___(12) garage. Then he called ___a___(13) taxi to take him to work. He had

___an___(14) important meeting with ___a___(15) top client. But Sam was late and he missed

___the___(16) appointment and lost ___the___(17) client.

25

Discussing Transportation Issues

A Read the flight information and answer the questions below.

FLIGHT SCHEDULE ✈

Select Your Departing Flight for Fri., Sept. 1, 2012

Price	Departing	Arriving	Travel Time	Flight Number
$242.00	1:55 P.M. New York, NY (LGA)	3:07 P.M. Philadelphia, PA (PHL)	1hr 12min	321
	Change Planes. Connect time in Philadelphia, PA (PHL) is 3 hours 3 minutes.			
	6:10 P.M. Philadelphia, PA (PHL)	9:13 P.M. Miami, FL (MIA)	3hr 3min	265
$195.00 Non-stop	2:22 P.M. New York, NY (LGA)	5:26 P.M. Miami, FL (MIA)	3hr 4min	488
$517.30	6:40 A.M. New York, NY (LGA)	8:18 A.M. Cleveland, OH (CLE)	1hr 38min	544
	Change Planes. Connect time in Cleveland, OH (CLE) is 1 hour 2 minutes.			
	9:20 A.M. Cleveland, OH (CLE)	12:11 P.M. Miami, FL (MIA)	2hr 51min	299

1. Which flight or flights take the most time to get from New York to Miami? _____

2. Which flight or flights take the least time to get from New York to Miami? _____

3. Which flights have the longer layover between connecting flights? _____

4. Which flight is the least expensive? _____

5. Which flight or flights are the best deal? Why? _____

_____

B Complete these conversations using the flight information above.

1. A: Can you tell me when flight 488 leaves New York?

   B: Yes. It leaves New York at _____

2. A: Can you tell me when flight 299 arrives in Miami?

   B: _____

3. A: Can you tell me how long the flight between Philadelphia and Miami is?

   B: _____

4. A: Do you know how long the layover in Cleveland is?

   B: _____

C Rewrite the direct questions below as indirect questions. Then answer them. Use your imagination.

HW
5/10

1. What caused the car accident?

   Indirect question: _Do you know what caused the accident?_

   Answer: _____

2. What time of day did the accident happen?

   Indirect question: _____?

   Answer: _____.

3. Was the car damaged?

   Indirect question: _____?

   Answer: _____.

4. Did anyone get hurt?

   Indirect question: _____?

   Answer: _____.

5. Did an ambulance come?

   Indirect question: _____?

   Answer: _____.

6. How many people were in the car?

   Indirect question: _____?

   Answer: _____.

7. Who was driving?

   Indirect question: _____?

   Answer: _____.

8. Did the driver have insurance?

   Indirect question: _____?

   Answer: _____.

Dealing With Emergencies

A Test your knowledge of workers' health and safety by taking the quiz below. Check (✓) your guesses. Then go to page 184 to see the answers.

Workers' Health and Safety Quiz

1. Workers in the United States have certain basic health and safety rights. Which of the following is NOT one of your rights at work?

   ☐ to remove uncomfortable safety equipment

   ☐ to report safety problems to OSHA (Occupational Safety & Health Administration)

   ☐ to get payment for medical care if you get hurt on the job

   ☐ to get health and safety training

   ☐ to see the record of injuries at your workplace

2. The most common workplace injuries are _____.

   ☐ chemical burns   ☐ cuts, lacerations

   ☐ fractures   ☐ sprains, strains

3. True or False? Your boss can fire you for refusing to do unsafe work.

   ☐ true   ☐ false

4. Which industry has the most workplace fatalities?

   ☐ construction   ☐ automotive

   ☐ mining   ☐ farming

5. True or False? Office workers don't have to worry about getting injured at work.

   ☐ true   ☐ false

B Read questions 1 to 5. Then read the story on page 29 and look for answers to the questions. Write your answers in complete sentences on the lines below.

1. How did James Wright get hurt?

   _____

2. How serious were his injuries?

   _____

3. How old is he now?

   _____

4. What advice does Wright have for workers?

   _____

5. Why do you think Wright didn't ask his boss for safety training?

   _____

I Don't Remember Hitting the Ground

James Wright
Ottawa, Canada

I got a job as an apprentice tinsmith[1] and was earning high school credits. Two weeks into the job, I fell fifty feet—five stories—off a ladder and now I'm paralyzed[2] from the waist down. I was eighteen when it happened.

As it stands now, I'll be in a wheelchair for the rest of my life. The fall shattered my lower spine and six years later I'm still in a lot of pain. Usually I can only get three to five hours of sleep a night.

Getting hurt like I did, there are lots of things you miss out on. I was very active. I played a lot of sports. Now what I miss most is being able to go out and live free—I find that I'm always dependent on somebody.

After all that's happened, I don't feel resentful[3]. I have a better understanding of what I lost and what I still have. I feel grateful to be alive. An accident like that can happen so easily, at the snap of your fingers. So if you don't feel safe, tell your boss and ask for training. I never received any proper safety training. If I had, I might not have fallen off that ladder.

Source: From "I don't remember hitting the ground." James Wright—Ottawa from www.yworker.com. Reprinted with permission of Ontario's Workplace Safety and Insurance Board.

---

[1] tinsmith: person who makes things from tin or other light metals
[2] paralyzed: unable to move
[3] resentful: angry or hurt

C Write sentences. Use the cues in parentheses and a modal (*may, might, could, should,* or *ought to*). More than one answer may be correct.

1. (possible: That car has its hazard lights on.)

_____

2. (probable: I just called the police. They will be here in five minutes.)

_____

3. (possible: I forgot to get gas before we left.)

_____

4. (probable: There isn't much traffic. We are five miles from the airport, and our flight leaves in two hours.)

_____

_____

D Read the situations. Make logical conclusions with *must*. Different answers are possible.

1. Diana was up all night last night because her son was sick. Now she is at work.

_____

2. Jim has a lot of vacation time, but he never travels anywhere.

_____

3. Bob has had three accidents this year.

_____

4. Mary is buying a new car.

_____

Reading: Identifying the Topic and Main Idea

A Read each paragraph below and identify the topic and the main idea.

1

The last trip I took was in 2006. That year I went to Italy to visit my brother. I thought this would be a great trip, but in fact, it was pretty awful. The worst thing that happened was that my brother got the flu and he had to stay in bed the whole time I was there. Besides that, the airlines lost my luggage on the flight over, so for the first three days of my trip, I didn't have any clean clothes to put on. And then, to top it off, it rained every day I was there.

Topic: _____

Main Idea:

_____

_____

_____

2

Yesterday a car pulled into the road right in front of me. The driver was talking on his cell phone, and he never even saw me. It was only because I stepped on the brake that I was able to avoid an accident. Another time I was driving on the highway and a car passed me going quite fast. When I looked at the driver, I noticed that he was shaving his face! It's amazing the stupid things people will do while they are driving.

Topic: _____

Main Idea:

_____

_____

_____

3

There are many different ways to get around in the United States. Many cities have buses, trains (or "subways"), trolleys, or streetcars. For a small fee, you can ride these vehicles. In some places, you can buy a card good for several trips on subways or buses. You can also pay for each trip separately. Taxicabs, or "taxis," are cars that take you where you want to go for a fee. Taxis are more expensive than other types of public transportation.

Topic: _____

Main Idea:

_____

_____

_____

4

Owning a car is a convenient way to get around, but it's expensive, too. In addition to paying for the car, you have to pay for car insurance and registration. You also have to pay for car maintenance and repairs. And don't forget the cost of gasoline, parking, and tolls. It's important to think of all the costs before you decide to buy a car.

Topic: _____

Main Idea:

_____

_____

_____

B Read the article. What is the topic and main idea of each paragraph? Write your answers in the chart below.

Save Money on Gasoline

1   Do you wish you could spend less money on gasoline for your automobile? You can. All you have to do is follow a few simple rules of car ownership.

2   One of the easiest ways to save money on gasoline is just to change the way you drive. If you drive fewer miles, you will spend less on gasoline. However, if this isn't possible, you can also reduce the amount of money you spend on gasoline by driving more slowly. By reducing your speed just 5 to 10 miles per hour below the speed limit, you could improve your fuel efficiency by 10 percent. That translates into a substantial savings.

3   Checking the air pressure in your tires can make a difference in fuel efficiency. Tires lose pressure over time, forcing the engine of the car to work harder to push the vehicle forward. That translates into lower gas mileage and more money spent on gasoline. Check your tire pressure regularly and you will save money on gasoline.

4   Keeping your car in good condition with regular tune-ups can also help you save money on gasoline. For example, regularly changing the fuel filter prevents dirt from collecting in the fuel tank. This can help you to get the best possible gas mileage.

5   You can also save money on gas by improving the aerodynamics of your car. Roof racks, for example, create air turbulence, which decreases fuel efficiency. Carrying heavy things in your car will do the same.

6   Another way to save money on gasoline is to pay attention to when you fill up the tank. Most people wait until their gas tank is almost empty before they fill it up again. However, this can cause dirt in the tank to pass into the fuel filter. You might get better gas mileage if you refill the gas tank when it still has a quarter of a tank of gas.

Paragraph	Topic	Main Idea
1		
2		
3		
4		
5		
6		

Writing: Using Compound Subjects, Verbs and Objects

A Add information from the box to each sentence below.

Nouns		Verbs
snow	signals	speeding
bumpers	car safety seats	register
liability	ambulance	concentrating
driver's license	driving test	

1. Cars have to have a windshield.

   Cars have to have a windshield and bumpers.

2. You can get a traffic ticket for parking illegally.

3. Would you mind turning down the radio?

4. You should drive extra carefully in fog.

5. It's important to have collision coverage.

6. You should obey all traffic laws.

7. Pull over to the side of the road if a police car wants to pass you.

8. You must take a vision test before you can get a driver's license.

9. If you own a car, you have to pay to insure it.

10. Your insurance card must be with you whenever you drive.

B Combine each pair of sentences, using *and* or *but*.

1. Karla doesn't have a driver's license yet. She is taking driving lessons now.

   _____

2. Joel can afford to buy a car. He can't afford to pay for car insurance.

   _____

3. You should change the oil in your car regularly. You should keep your tires properly inflated.

   _____

4. You should obey the speed limit. You should always wear your seatbelt.

   _____

5. You can rent a car instead of buying one. It's expensive to rent a car.

   _____

6. You can get a cheap flight if you are willing to make several stops. It can take a long time to get to your destination.

   _____

   _____

7. It's convenient to own a car. It's expensive to own a car.

   _____

8. You can buy a new car. A new car depreciates quickly.

   _____

C Rewrite the body of the letter below. Make the writing smoother by combining sentences.

September 12, 2012

Dear Sam,

   I want you to know that I feel terrible about the damage done to your car. I want to take full responsibility for repairing it.
   It was very thoughtful of you to say it was minor damage. I won't feel good until it is fixed. I hope you won't mind that I called Dan's Garage. I asked them to look at the damage and give an estimate.
   Please accept my apologies. I hope this will not affect our friendship.

My best,

Josh

Family: Recreational Events

A Read the Calendar of Events and circle the 3 most interesting activities. Then write a sentence telling why each activity is interesting to you.

EXAMPLE: *I'm interested in the Summer Insects program because it's free and my children like to do things outdoors.*

1. _____
   _____

2. _____
   _____

3. _____
   _____

CALENDAR OF EVENTS

Concerts

Canoga Park High School – "Wayne from Maine," family concert, Saturday, 1 P.M. $6/adults, $4/kids. Info: 555-3838.

Hollywood Community Music School, Glendale – Youth Symphony Orchestra, Saturday, 7 P.M. Info: 555-8839.

Palace Theater, Alhambra – Palace Youth Theater presents *Schoolhouse Rock, Live* at 7 P.M. Friday and 10 A.M. Saturday. Info: 555-9088.

Theater

Glendale High School, Glendale – *The King and I,* Friday, 7 P.M. free. Info: 555-4394.

Burbank – The Tamborines, folk dancers, Saturday, 8 P.M., Dana Center. Info: 555-3030.

Town Hall, Pacoima – Weekend Family Series begins at 2 P.M. on Sunday. Circle Comedy Clowns. Tickets are $5. Info: 555-2142.

Speakers

Glendale Town Hall, Glendale – "An Afternoon of Humor," with Sandra Hale, Sunday, 2 P.M. Info: 555-3383.

Books

Turner Bookstore, Van Nuys – Storytime, Saturday, 11 A.M. Info: 555-3993.

Arleta Public Library, Arleta – "Lapsit," stories, rhymes, and songs, through age 2, Fridays, 10 A.M. "Books at Bedtime," story program for all ages, Fridays, 7 P.M. Free programs. Info: 555-4993.

Outdoors

Glendale Nature Center, Glendale – "Summer Insects," family program, Sunday, 1:30 P.M. Free. Registration required. Info: 555-4753.

Silk Farm, North Hollywood – For kids/families, "The Masked Bandit," Saturday, 9:30–11 A.M. Program for preschoolers and an accompanying adult. $3/$5, Registration required. Info: 555-7798.

B Use the information in the Calendar of Events in Activity A to answer the questions.

1. How many of the activities are free? _____

2. How many of the activities require registration?
   _____

3. How many of the activities are especially for children and families? _____

4. If a family of 2 adults and 3 children wanted to go to the program at the Silk Farm in North Hollywood, how much would it cost? _____

5. A family of 6 (two adults and four children ages 6, 8, 9, and 11) is looking for something to do on Saturday. Which program would you recommend? Why?

_____

_____

_____

C The activities in the calendar on page 34 are organized by type. Reorganize them by day of the week.

Activities on Friday	Activities on Saturday	Activities on Sunday
Schoolhouse Rock, Live	"Wayne from Maine" family concert	

TAKE IT OUTSIDE: LOOK IN LOCAL NEWSPAPERS TO FIND LISTINGS OF EVENTS IN YOUR AREA. BRING THE LISTINGS TO CLASS AND SHARE WHAT YOU LEARNED.

Work: Directions

A Study the map and circle the answer that best completes each sentence.

1. Trenton is _____ of Mercerville.
   A. northwest
   B. southeast
   C. southwest

2. Penn Valley is directly _____ of Sylvan Glen.
   A. east
   B. north
   C. west

3. Mercerville is _____ of Morrisville.
   A. northeast
   B. northwest
   C. southeast

4. Route 295 runs parallel to Route _____.
   A. 1
   B. 195
   C. 29

5. Route 29 crosses Route _____.
   A. 13
   B. 195
   C. 1

6. Route 29 becomes Route _____.
   A. 1
   B. 295
   C. 195

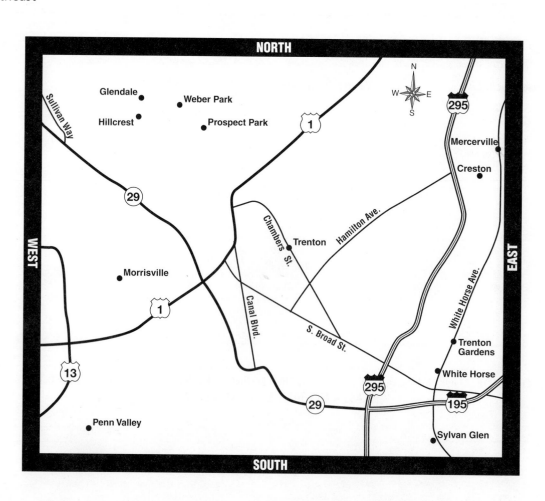

B Read each situation. Then use the map on page 36 to complete the directions to each place of work. Circle the correct answer.

1. Situation: You work at a store on the northeast corner of Canal Blvd. and S. Broad St. A customer wants directions to the store from the intersection of Route 13 and Route 1.

   Directions: Go (north/south) on Route 1. When you get to S. Broad St. turn (right/left). The store is on the (left/right) side of S. Broad Street.

2. Situation: Your office is on the northeastern side of Sullivan Way. A salesperson asks you for directions to your office from Creston.

   Directions: Get onto Route 295 going (north/south/east/west). Continue on 295 until you get to (Route 1/ Route 29). Go (east/west). After (Route 1/Route 13), look for the exit for Sullivan Way. The office is about a mile up on the right side of Sullivan Way.

3. Situation: A truck driver needs to get to your place of business in Trenton Gardens. He calls you on his cell phone and says that he is in Penn Valley right now.

   Directions: You want to get on Route 13 going (north/south). When you get to Route (1/29), go north. Stay on this road until you get to Route 29 where you want to go (east/west). After Route 29 crosses Route 295, it becomes Route (13/195). Stay on this road until you see the sign for White Horse Avenue. Go (north/south) on White Horse until you come to Trenton Gardens. The company is on the right on White Horse Avenue.

C Write the directions from Sylvan Glen to your place of work in Weber Park.

_____

_____

_____

_____

_____

_____

_____

_____

_____

_____

TAKE IT OUTSIDE: INTERVIEW A CLASSMATE. FIND OUT THE PERSON'S HOME OR WORK ADDRESS AND ASK FOR DIRECTIONS FROM THEIR HOME OR WORK TO YOUR SCHOOL.

Practice Test

DIRECTIONS: Read the insurance bill to answer the next 4 questions. Use the Answer Sheet.

Bob Jones Automobile Insurance Co.
4695 Breyer Road
Culver City, CA 90232

STATEMENT

| Payment DUE DATE 10-01-11 |

TO CHANGE A POLICY, CALL
1-800-555-3594
FOR BILLING QUESTIONS, CALL
1-800-467-9377
TO REPORT A CLAIM, CALL
1-800-569-5699

VICTOR DANKO
552 MONTEREY BLVD.
Montebello, CA 90640

POLICY PERIOD
OCT-01-11 TO APR-01-12

DESCRIBED VEHICLE

MAKE	YEAR	BODY STYLE	VEHICLE IDENTIFICATION NUMBER	PREMIUM FOR THIS POLICY PERIOD
MAZDA	2006	4DR	3B356AW49499	$385.30

---

1. Who is being insured with this policy?

   A. Bob Jones

   B. Mazda 02

   C. Victor Danko

   D. none of the above

2. When is a payment due?

   A. October 10, 2009

   B. January 10, 2008

   C. October 1, 2011

   D. May 1, 2010

3. How long is this policy in effect?

   A. one month

   B. six months

   C. one year

   D. two years

4. What is the annual premium for this policy?

   A. $28.60

   B. $385.30

   C. $770.60

   D. $858.40

ANSWER SHEET

	A	B	C	D
1	A	B	C	D
2	A	B	C	D
3	A	B	C	D
4	A	B	C	D
5	A	B	C	D
6	A	B	C	D
7	A	B	C	D
8	A	B	C	D
9	A	B	C	D
10	A	B	C	D

DIRECTIONS: Read the information about reporting an accident to answer the next 6 questions. Use the Answer Sheet on page 38.

When you are required to report an accident to DMV

If you are involved in a vehicle accident that occurred in California, you must report it to DMV if:
- there was property damage of more than $750 **or**
- anyone was injured (no matter how minor) **or** killed.

Each driver must make a report to DMV within 10 days, whether you caused the accident or not, and even if the accident occurred on private property.

You must complete a DMV Traffic Accident Report form SR 1/SR 1A.

When you have completed the form, you can mail it to:

    Department of Motor Vehicles
    Financial Responsibility (Mail Station J-237)
    PO Box 942884
    Sacramento, California 94284-0884

If you do not submit this report, your driving privilege will be suspended. DMV may ask your insurance company to verify that you had coverage in effect at the time of the accident. If you did not have insurance, your driving privilege will be suspended for one year. To get your license back after the suspension, you will need to provide proof of financial responsibility and maintain it on record for three years. The accident may count as one point on your driving record (California Insurance Requirements).

Source: http://www.dmv.ca.gov/

---

5. Who do these instructions apply to?
   A. California residents only
   B. anyone who is driving in California
   C. California residents over the age of 70
   D. all uninsured motorists

6. Which of the following topics is included in the instructions for reporting an accident?
   A. who needs to report an accident
   B. how long you have to report an accident
   C. what happens after you report the accident
   D. all of the above

7. According to the article above, when don't you have to report an accident?
   A. when no one was hurt seriously
   B. when no one was injured and damages were $750 or less
   C. when there was no one in the other car
   D. when you are a resident of a state other than California

8. According to the article above, which of the following statements is true?
   A. You don't have to file an accident report if there was no damage and no one was hurt.
   B. You don't have to file a report if the accident took place on your driveway.
   C. You have to pay a fine if you send your report late.
   D. You have two weeks to report an accident.

9. According to the article above, which of the following statements is true?
   A. You should report an accident by calling the Department of Motor Vehicles.
   B. Only the driver who caused the accident should file a report.
   C. If you don't have insurance, you will lose your driver's license for a month.
   D. You have ten days to report an accident.

10. What form should you use to report an accident in California?
   A. Form J-237
   B. Form 94284
   C. Form SR /
   D. Form SR 1/SR 1A

HOW DID YOU DO? Count the number of correct answers on your answer sheet. Record this number in the bar graph on the inside back cover.

Describing a Health Emergency

A Write the past tense of each verb.

1. take _____
2. feel _____
3. fall _____
4. arrive _____
5. ride _____
6. give _____

7. run _____
8. collapse _____
9. bring _____
10. see _____
11. say _____
12. get _____

B Combine the information in each pair of sentences with *and* or *but*.

1. Oscar was at home when he got sick. His wife was there, too.

_____

2. Oscar tried to stand up. He fell to the floor.

_____

3. Oscar's wife ran to the phone. She quickly called 911.

_____

4. An ambulance rushed to Oscar's house. Oscar didn't want to go to the hospital.

_____

5. The EMTs put Oscar in the ambulance. They put an oxygen mask on his face.

_____

_____

6. Oscar rode to the hospital in the back of the ambulance. His wife followed in their car.

_____

_____

7. A doctor gave Oscar some medicine. A nurse took his vital signs.

_____

8. Oscar wanted to leave the hospital. The doctor said he should stay there for several days.

_____

_____

9. There was plenty of food to eat at the hospital. Oscar wasn't very hungry.

_____

_____

10. After a week, Oscar felt much better. The doctors said he could go home.

_____

C Read the information and answer the questions.

When Should You Go to the Emergency Room?

At 7 in the morning, Ted suddenly felt a squeezing pain in the center of his chest. The pain then spread to his shoulders, neck, and arms. Ted thought he was going to faint, so he called to his wife, Nancy. Nancy wanted to call for an ambulance, but Ted asked her to wait awhile. Thirty minutes later, Ted didn't feel any better, so he asked Nancy to drive him to the hospital. By the time they arrived at the hospital, Ted was having trouble breathing. By the time Nancy stopped the car at the entrance to the emergency room, Ted was having a major heart attack. Nancy says she wishes she had called 911 and gotten Ted to the hospital right away, but like most people, Ted didn't want to go, and Nancy wasn't sure it was an emergency situation.

It's not always easy to know when to go to the emergency room, but if you are in doubt, it's always better to be safe than sorry. In most areas, you should dial 911 if you think someone needs emergency help. For some kinds of emergencies, every minute can make the difference between life and death, so don't delay.

If you take someone with a non-life-threatening problem to the emergency room, you can help make sure the patient is taken care of properly. The patient will need to check in with the triage nurse in the emergency room. The triage nurse will assess the patient's condition to determine how serious it is. The patient will also need to provide information about his or her medical history, drug allergies, medications, and health insurance coverage. While you are waiting in the emergency room, you should also watch for any changes in the patient's condition; let the nurse know if the person seems to be getting worse.

1. What were Ted's symptoms?

_____

_____

2. What should Nancy have done?

_____

_____

3. What does a triage nurse do?

_____

_____

4. What information do patients need to provide when they go to the emergency room?

_____

_____

Identifying Health Care Professionals

A Complete each sentence with the name of the correct health care professional.

Health Care Professionals

cardiologist	primary care physician	optometrist
chiropractor	physical therapist	pediatrician
dermatologist	obstetrician	psychiatrist

1. An _____ specializes in eye diseases.

2. After an accident, you should make an appointment with
   a _____.

3. If you have a rash or itchy skin, you should see a _____.

4. Neither a physical therapist nor a _____ is a medical
   doctor.

5. If you have a family history of heart disease, your _____
   might refer you to a _____.

6. If your child has an earache, you can take her to a _____.

7. If you lose interest in everything around you, you might want to see a _____.

8. An _____ delivers babies.

B Complete the paragraph. Use the present perfect continuous form of the verb in parentheses.
Use contractions or full forms.

Kim ___*has been volunteering*___ (volunteer) at a hospital since the beginning of the summer. She and two
①

other students _____ (work) there three days a week. Kim is happy to be working
②

there because she _____ (think) about studying nursing. The nurses
③

_____ (keep) her busy. Kim _____ (make) beds, she
④ ⑤

_____ (talk) with the patients, and she _____ (read) to the
⑥ ⑦

children. Her favorite patient is a twelve year old, Maria Salas. Maria has been in the hospital for two months,

but everyone thinks that she _____ (get) better since Kim started working there. Kim
⑧

is not sure about that, but she knows that she and the other volunteers _____ (get)
⑨

valuable experience at the hospital.

B Use the information in the article and your background knowledge to answer the questions.

Medical Records and Health Information Technicians

Significant Points
- This is one of the few health occupations in which there is little or no direct contact with patients.
- Medical records and health information technicians entering the field usually have an associate's degree; courses include anatomy, physiology, medical terminology, and computer science.
- Job prospects should be very good, particularly in offices of physicians.

Nature of the Work

Every time a patient receives health care, a record is maintained of the observations, medical or surgical interventions, and treatment outcomes. This record includes information that the patient provides concerning his or her symptoms and medical history, the results of examinations, reports of x-rays and laboratory tests, diagnoses, and treatment plans. Medical records and health information technicians organize and evaluate these records for completeness and accuracy.

Technicians begin to assemble patients' health information by first making sure their initial medical charts are complete. They ensure that all forms are completed and properly identified and signed, and that all necessary information is in the computer. They regularly communicate with physicians or other health care professionals to clarify diagnoses or to obtain additional information.

Working Conditions

Medical records and health information technicians usually work a 40-hour week. Some overtime may be required. In hospitals—where health information departments are often open 24 hours a day, 7 days a week—technicians may work day, evening, and night shifts.

Medical records and health information technicians work in pleasant and comfortable offices. Because accuracy is essential in their jobs, technicians must pay close attention to detail. Technicians who work at computer monitors for prolonged periods must guard against eyestrain and muscle pain.

Source: Excerpted from the U.S. government Occupational Handbook

---

1. What are 4 tasks that health information technicians do?

   - _____   - _____

   - _____   - _____

2. What skills do health information technicians need to have? _____

3. Why do health information technicians need to have good communication skills? _____

   _____

4. What would you like and dislike about this type of work? Complete the chart below.

Things I would like about the job:	Things I would dislike about the job:

Calling the Doctor's Office

A Number each conversation in order starting with #1. Then add the information from the conversations to the appointment calendar below.

Conversation A

_____ Yes, the fifth would work fine.

_____ I'm calling to set up an appointment.

_____ Yes. It's 555-9904.

_____ I'm sorry, that was the 15th, not the 5th.

_____ Your name please?

_____ Yes, that's right. Can I have your phone number, please?

_____ Could you come in at noon on the 15th, Ms. James?

_____ The 15th? Oh, that's fine too. You said noon?

___1___ Dr. Ray's Office. How can I help you?

_____ It's James. Beverly James.

Conversation B

_____ Okay. Let me look for a morning appointment. What about the 15th at 8:30?

_____ And when would you like to come in?

_____ Hello, this is Chris Ma calling. I need to change an appointment I have with Dr. Ray.

_____ And when is your appointment?

___1___ Dr. Ray's office.

_____ It's this coming Friday at nine.

_____ That would be perfect.

_____ Does she have any openings next week?

_____ No, that won't work. I can only come in the morning.

_____ Let me see. Yes, she has an opening on the 12th at 2. Would you like that?

Conversation C

_____ I think it was 11 o'clock.

_____ What day was your appointment?

_____ Yes, this is Juanita Perez calling. I need to cancel an appointment.

_____ And the time?

_____ It was on the 15th.

_____ Yes, I see it now. Do you want to reschedule that?

___1___ Dr. Ray's office. Can I help you?

_____ Not right now, thank you. I'll call back later.

Appointments Calendar ⊠ ⊟ ⊞

Date: May 15, 2011 ▼   **Doctor:** Ray, Sylvia ▼

Start Time	Patient's Name	Procedure	Home Phone
08:30			
09:00	Oscar Hernandez	Follow-up	555-8574
09:30	Paul Smith	VAC	555-4586
10:00			
10:30	Sara Chang	EXAM	555-4733
11:00	Juanita Perez	Regular Visit	555-9955
11:30			
12:00			
12:30			

B Use the appointment calendar on page 44 to answer the questions below.

1. How many appointments does Dr. Ray now have on the 15th? _____

2. When is Ms. Chang's appointment? _____

3. What is the purpose of Oscar's appointment? _____

4. How much time does Dr. Ray spend with each patient? _____

5. According to this calendar, when will Dr. Ray finish seeing her last patient on the 15th? _____

C Complete the conversation. Use the gerund or the infinitive form of the verb in parentheses.

Ray: Hi Paul, I didn't see you on the trail this morning.

Paul: I haven't been feeling well lately. I usually enjoy _____ (run) in the morning, but lately

　　　 I haven't been able _____ (get) up early enough.
　　　　　　　　　　　　　　　②

Ray: Have you considered _____ (take) vitamins?
　　　　　　　　　　　　　③

Paul: I guess I could try _____ (do) that. Are they expensive?
　　　　　　　　　　　④

Ray: I recommend _____ (buy) them online because they are cheaper. If you want
　　　　　　　　　⑤

　　　 _____ (start) today, I have some at home.
　　　　　⑥

Paul: Thanks, but I prefer _____ (buy) my own.
　　　　　　　　　　　⑦

Ray: You know, you look pretty tired. You might also consider _____ (get) more sleep.
　　　　　　　　　　　　　　　　　　　　　　　　　　⑧

Paul: You're right. I'd like _____ (get) to bed earlier, but I have _____
　　　　　　　　　　⑨　　　　　　　　　　　　　　　　　　　　　　　　⑩

　　　 (study) at night.

Ray: Well, if you're not out running next week, I recommend _____ (see) a doctor
　　　　　　　　　　　　　　　　　　　　　　　　　　　　　⑪

　　　 and _____ (have) a physical exam.
　　　　　　⑫

Paul: Thanks for the advice, Ray. I hope _____ (feel) well enough to run next week. If I don't,
　　　　　　　　　　　　　　　　　　　⑬

　　　 though, I promise _____ (see) a doctor.
　　　　　　　　　　⑭

Interpreting Nutritional Information

A Read this information and the statements on page 47. Check (✓) *True* or *False*.

Q: Why are fruits and vegetables important for my health?

A: This year in the United States, more than 1.4 million Americans will be diagnosed with cancer and over 500,000 Americans will die of cancer. An estimated 32% of these deaths may be related to diet. Fruit and vegetable intake is an important part of a healthy diet that may reduce risk of cancer. The health benefits of fruits and vegetables go beyond cancer prevention. During recent decades, studies examining the relationship between dietary patterns and health have found that a diet rich in fruits and vegetables has been associated with the prevention of heart disease, the leading cause of death in the U.S., as well.

Q: How many fruits and vegetables should be eaten daily for good health?

A: The National Academy of Sciences, U.S. Department of Agriculture (USDA), the National Cancer Institute, and the American Cancer Society recommend that 5 to 9 servings of fruits and vegetables be consumed each day depending on a person's energy intake, to reduce risk of cancer and maintain good health. Many adults should be eating closer to 9 daily servings for maximum health benefits!

Source: http://www.cdc.gov/

	True	False
1. More than a million people in the U.S. will learn that they have cancer this year.	☐	☐
2. All deaths from cancer are related to poor diet.	☐	☐
3. Eating fruits and vegetables may help to prevent cancer.	☐	☐
4. Eating a lot of fruit and vegetables will not help prevent heart disease.	☐	☐
5. The American Cancer Society recommends that people eat 3 to 5 servings of fruits and vegetables daily.	☐	☐

B Study the food labels and answer the questions below.

REDUCED FAT MILK
2% Milkfat

Nutrition Facts
Serving Size 1 cup (236ml)
Servings Per Container 1

Amount Per Serving

Calories 120   Calories from Fat 45

	% Daily Value*
Total Fat 5g	8%
Saturated Fat 3g	15%
Trans Fat 0g	
Cholesterol 20mg	7%
Sodium 120mg	5%
Total Carbohydrate 11g	4%
Dietary Fiber 0g	0%
Sugars 11g	
Protein 9g	17%

Vitamin A 10% • Vitamin C 4%
Calcium 30% • Iron 0% • Vitamin D 25%

*Percent Daily Values are based on a 2,000 calorie diet. Your daily values may be higher or lower depending on your calorie needs.

CHOCOLATE NONFAT MILK

Nutrition Facts
Serving Size 1 cup (236ml)
Servings Per Container 1

Amount Per Serving

Calories 80   Calories from Fat 0

	% Daily Value*
Total Fat 0g	0%
Saturated Fat 0g	0%
Trans Fat 0g	
Cholesterol Less than 5mg	0%
Sodium 120mg	5%
Total Carbohydrate 11g	4%
Dietary Fiber 0g	0%
Sugars 11g	
Protein 9g	17%

Vitamin A 10% • Vitamin C 4%
Calcium 30% • Iron 0% • Vitamin D 25%

*Percent Daily Values are based on a 2,000 calorie diet. Your daily values may be higher or lower depending on your calorie needs.

1. How many servings are there in a container of reduced fat milk? _____

2. Which type of milk has more calories per serving—reduced fat milk or chocolate nonfat milk?

_____

3. Which has more fat per serving—reduced fat milk or chocolate nonfat milk? _____

4. Which has more cholesterol—reduced fat milk or chocolate nonfat milk? _____

5. How many cups of nonfat milk would you need to drink daily to get the recommended amount of Vitamin D? _____

Reading: Using Context Clues

A Read the definitions and the sentences. Use context clues to choose the correct definition for the word in each sentence. Circle the number of the definition.

> **fatigue** *noun*
>
> **1** extreme tiredness
>
> **2** *plural* military clothes
>
> **3** the weakening of a material due to stress

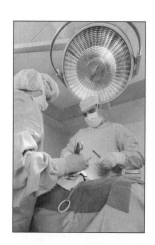

1. Poor eating habits can cause **fatigue**.   1 2 3
2. **Fatigue** is a common symptom of many illnesses.   1 2 3
3. The building collapsed because of metal **fatigue**.   1 2 3
4. In the army, he used to wear **fatigues**.   1 2 3

> **bill** *noun*
>
> **1** a written statement of the amount of money to be paid
>
> **2** a piece of paper money
>
> **3** a written proposal for a new law

5. Have you paid your **bills** yet?   1 2 3
6. The Senate is voting on the new health care **bill**.   1 2 3
7. Do you have a ten dollar **bill** on you?   1 2 3
8. How much was the hospital **bill**?   1 2 3

> **perform** *verb*
>
> **1** to carry out an action
>
> **2** to present or act in a performance such as a play, concert, or dance

9. He used to **perform** in plays.   1 2
10. They **performed** bravely in the emergency.   1 2
11. The doctor **performed** the surgery in just an hour.   1 2

B Read the information and use context clues to guess the meaning of the boldfaced words. Then match each word to a synonym in the chart below. Write the words on the lines.

> Q: How important are nutrition and dietary factors in health and chronic disease prevention?
>
> A: The Surgeon General's Report on Nutrition and Health in 1988 noted that 2/3 of all deaths are due to diseases **associated** with diet. The report also says that the three most important personal habits that **influence** health are smoking, alcohol consumption, and diet. For the two out of three adults who do not drink alcohol **excessively** or smoke, the single most important personal choice influencing long-term health is what they eat.
>
> In 1997, a report by the World Cancer Research Fund and the American Institute for Cancer Research stated that recommended diets **in conjunction** with physical activity and normal BMI (body mass index) could reduce cancer **incidence** by 30–40%.
>
> For heart disease, the report by the 1989 National Academy of Sciences **projected** that 20% of deaths could be avoided by reducing fats and increasing fruits, vegetables, breads, cereals, and legumes (dry beans and peas).

Source: http://www.cdc.gov/

Words from the article	**Synonyms**
1. associated _____connected_____	a. together
2. influence _____	b. connected
3. excessively _____	c. affect
4. in conjunction _____	d. frequency
5. incidence _____	e. too much
6. projected _____	f. predicted

C Use the article in Activity B to answer these questions.

1. What 3 things have the biggest negative effect on people's health?

_____

_____

2. In addition to eating healthy food, what does the article say you can do to reduce your risk of cancer?

_____

_____

Writing: Identifying Punctuation Marks

A Write the correct punctuation mark in each circle.

Taking Care of Your Health

People in the U.S. pay for their own medical care. Medical care is expensive ◯ so many people buy health insurance. It is important to get health insurance for yourself and your family.
1

Employers may offer health insurance as a benefit to their employees. Some employers pay all of your monthly health insurance fee ◯ and some pay only part of the fee. This monthly fee is called a "premium." You may need to pay part of the premium ◯ Usually ◯ employers deduct the employee's part of the premium from their paycheck.
2 **3** **4**

When you go to the doctor, you may have to pay a fee (often about $15-$20). This is called a "co-payment ◯"
5

Doctors send their bills to your health insurance company. The health insurance company pays for some or all of your medical bills.

If you do not have health insurance ◯ you may be able to get federal or state health care assistance. In general ◯ most states provide some type of assistance to children and pregnant women. Check with the public health department of your state or town.
6 **7**

If you need urgent medical care ◯ you can go to a hospital emergency room. Most hospitals are required by law to treat patients with a medical emergency even if the person can't pay.
8

Source: http://uscis.gov/

B Read the article in Activity A and answer the questions below.

1. Why is it important to buy health insurance in the United States?

_____

_____

2. What is a "co-payment"?

_____

_____

3. If you don't have medical insurance, what should you do if you have a medical emergency?

_____

_____

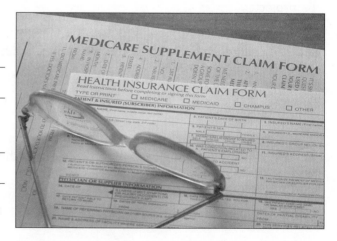

C Add the missing punctuation to the personal letters below.

September 12 2012

Dear Tricia

My apologies for not
returning your book sooner I
enjoyed it a lot and I thank
you for recommending it to me

Sincerely

Chandra

October 15 2013

Dear Phil and Ben

Please forgive me for not
writing sooner to thank you for
the beautiful flowers you sent
when I was in the hospital It
was very thoughtful of you to
think of me and having the
flowers cheered me up

My best
Oscar

D Write a letter to someone you know. Remember to punctuate your letter correctly.

Family: Feeling Sick

A Look at the words around the picture. Then use the words to complete the sentences.

1. A: Doctor, my _____ hurts. I think I ate something bad.

    B: Is the pain high or low in your abdomen? If it's low, it may be your _____.

2. A: I went on a long hike yesterday, and today my knees and ankles are stiff.

    B: Do you usually have stiffness in your _____ when you go hiking?

3. A: Both of my parents have high cholesterol. I'd like to make sure my cholesterol level isn't high. I don't want to have a _____ attack!

    B: Okay. I'll send you to the lab for a test. They'll take about a pint of _____ for the test.

4. A: I'm having trouble breathing.

    B: Let me listen to your _____. Take a deep breath. Now let it out slowly.

5. A: The _____ in my back are really tight and they ache. I lifted something heavy yesterday.

    B: I'll write you a prescription for the pain. And try not to lift anything heavy.

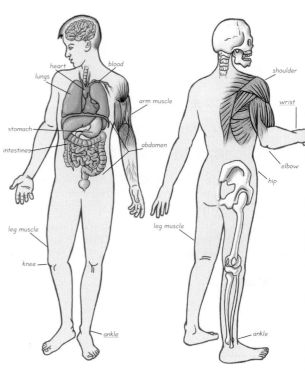

Labels: heart, blood, lungs, shoulder, arm muscle, wrist, stomach, intestines, abdomen, elbow, hip, leg muscle, leg muscle, knee, ankle, ankle

B **Conversation Challenge.** Practice the conversation below with a partner.

A: Good afternoon, Mr. Sawicki. How are you feeling today?

B: Not very well. I have a fever and my stomach hurts. My muscles ache, too.

A: I see.

B: I also cough all night and I can't sleep. My throat hurts from the coughing. It's hard to swallow.

A: Have you ever had any serious diseases?

B: I had a heart attack three years ago.

A: Are you taking any medications?

B: I'm taking cough syrup and a pain reliever. I'm also taking medication for high blood pressure and high cholesterol. I see a doctor every six months.

A: It sounds like you have the flu. You need to rest and drink a lot of water and juice. Are you allergic to any medications?

B: Yes. I'm allergic to penicillin.

C Practice the conversation in Activity B again. Replace the underlined words with your own ideas.

D Complete the form for Mr. Sawicki. Use the information in Activity B.

MEDICAL HISTORY FORM

Name: *Michael Sawicki*   Date: *November 22*

SYMPTOMS: Please check the symptoms you have now.

_____ fever	_____ pain in lungs	_____ joint pain
_____ blurry vision	_____ coughing	_____ back pain
_____ difficulty hearing	_____ coughing up blood	_____ skin problem
_____ difficulty swallowing	_____ pain in abdomen	_____ sleep problem
_____ trouble breathing	_____ muscle pain	_____ stress

MEDICATIONS: List all prescription and non-prescription medications.

Medication	Prescription (✓)	Over-the-Counter (✓)
_____	_____	_____
_____	_____	_____
_____	_____	_____

PERSONAL MEDICAL HISTORY: Check any of the medical problems you have had.

_____ heart disease	_____ high cholesterol	_____ cancer
_____ lung disease	_____ high blood pressure	_____ diabetes

ALLERGIES: List all medications that you are allergic to.

_____   _____   _____

MEDICAL CARE: Are you currently receiving medical care? Check one.

☐ Yes   ☐ No

If yes, what are you receiving care for? _____

Community: Emergencies

A Look at the words in the box. Circle these words on the drug label and in the patient education leaflet below. Then use the words to complete the sentences.

swelling	side effects	nausea	dizziness
fatigue	blurry	impair	persistent

1. I'm having trouble seeing. My vision is really unclear and _____.

2. Your medication might cause _____. Call your doctor if you feel sick to your stomach.

3. Three possible _____ of this medication are upset stomach, headache, and itching.

4. This drug may cause _____. Stand up carefully and don't turn your head too quickly.

5. Doctor, I'm experiencing _____ from my medication. I'm so sleepy all the time.

6. Is your headache _____? In other words, do you feel it constantly, all day long?

7. This pain medication might _____ your ability to make decisions. You shouldn't try to make any difficult decisions while you're taking this drug.

8. If you notice any _____ of your tongue, call me immediately. If it gets bad, you may have difficulty breathing. You could even choke.

WARNINGS:
- MAY CAUSE DIZZINESS.
- THIS DRUG MAY IMPAIR YOUR ABILITY TO DRIVE OR OPERATE MACHINERY.
- DO NOT TAKE THIS DRUG IF YOU ARE PREGNANT OR NURSING.

Patient Education Leaflet

PARSINIL 10 MG TABLETS

SIDE EFFECTS: You may experience dizziness when you stand quickly after sitting. You may also experience fatigue, occasional nausea, or blurry vision. If any of these effects continues for longer than 24 hours, call your doctor. Contact your doctor immediately if you experience any of these unlikely but serious side effects or allergic reactions: infection, persistent nausea (you feel sick for longer than three days), persistent fatigue (you are extremely tired for longer than three days), rash, trouble breathing, painful swelling of the feet so that your shoes don't fit.

B Complete insurance claim form for the man in Activity B. Use the information from the insurance card and the telephone conversation.

A: 911. What's the address of the emergency?

B: MY address is 917 West Street in Pasadena.

A: OK. Now please try to stay calm and tell me what's wrong.

B: My husband got dizzy and fell. He hit his head on the floor.

A: Is he conscious?

B: Yes, he is. But his breath is very weak.

A: Is he bleeding?

B: Yes, he is. His head is bleeding.

★★★ Lucky Stars Health Insurance

Member: **George Martinez**
DOB: **12/05/1962**

Patient ID Number: **7784-92732**

Customer Service: **1-800-555-3232**
In emergencies call 911

PATIENT INFORMATION

Insurance ID Number (Copy from your Lucky Stars Health Identification Card.) _____

Patient's Name: Sex: Date of Birth:

_____   ☐ Male ☐ Female   ___ / ___ / ___

CLAIM INFORMATION

Is the claim for

an accidental injury?   ☐ yes ☐ no

a car accident?   ☐ yes ☐ no

an employment accident   ☐ yes ☐ no

other   ☐ yes ☐ no

Which state did the accident occur in? _____

Date of accident: _____ 3/17/12 _____

Briefly describe the injury: _____

_____

_____

_____

Practice Test

DIRECTIONS: Read the food label to answer the next 6 questions. Use the Answer Sheet.

INGREDIENTS: ROASTED PEANUTS, CORN SYRUP SOLIDS, SUGAR, SOY PROTEIN, SALT, VEGETABLE OIL.

Nutrition Facts

Serving Size 2 Tbsp

Servings Per Container about 14

Amount Per Serving

Calories 190	Calories from Fat 100

	% Daily Value
Total Fat 12g	19%
Saturated Fat 2.5g	12%
Cholesterol 0mg	0%
Sodium 190 mg	8%
Total Carbohydrate 15g	5%
Protein 7g	

ANSWER SHEET

1 Ⓐ Ⓑ Ⓒ Ⓓ
2 Ⓐ Ⓑ Ⓒ Ⓓ
3 Ⓐ Ⓑ Ⓒ Ⓓ
4 Ⓐ Ⓑ Ⓒ Ⓓ
5 Ⓐ Ⓑ Ⓒ Ⓓ
6 Ⓐ Ⓑ Ⓒ Ⓓ
7 Ⓐ Ⓑ Ⓒ Ⓓ
8 Ⓐ Ⓑ Ⓒ Ⓓ
9 Ⓐ Ⓑ Ⓒ Ⓓ
10 Ⓐ Ⓑ Ⓒ Ⓓ

1. Which of these is not an ingredient in this peanut butter?

   A. peanuts   C. salt
   B. butter   D. sugar

2. How large is one serving of peanut butter?

   A. 2 teaspoons   C. 2 cups
   B. 2 tablespoons   D. 2 pints

3. How many grams of fat are there in a serving of this peanut butter?

   A. 2.5   C. 12
   B. 23   D. 0

4. About how many servings are there in this jar of peanut butter?

   A. 2   C. 100
   B. 14   D. 190

5. If you ate this whole jar of peanut butter, about how many calories would you consume?

   A. 190   C. 2660
   B. 380   D. 5320

6. This peanut butter does not contain any _____.

   A. salt   C. carbohydrates
   B. sugar   D. cholesterol

DIRECTIONS: Read the information below to answer the next 4 questions. Use the Answer Sheet on page 56.

Doctors are sometimes said to fall into two main groups: primary care physicians (sometimes referred to as generalists) and specialists. The term *primary care* refers to the medical fields that treat most common health problems—family medicine, pediatrics, and in some cases obstetrics and gynecology.

Specialists concentrate on particular types of illnesses or problems that affect specific tissues or organ systems in the body. They may treat patients with complicated illnesses who are referred to them by primary care physicians or by other specialists.

Whatever their focus, all physicians must hold one of two degrees. Most have an M.D. (doctor of medicine) degree, and some hold a D.O. (doctor of osteopathy) degree. The two types of degrees reflect different theories and practices of medicine, but medical licensing authorities recognize both types of doctors.

Doctors may hold many other degrees as well as medical degrees. Some have Ph.D. (doctor of philosophy) or master's degrees in the sciences or in fields like public health, hospital administration, or education.

Source: http://www.vh.org/

7. What is the topic of this article?
   A. medical specialties
   B. theories of medicine
   C. types of doctors
   D. primary care physicians

8. Which statement is true about all specialists?
   A. They have Ph.Ds.
   B. They hold a D.O. degree.
   C. They refer patients to primary care physicians.
   D. They have extra training in one area.

9. According to the article, which of these is a specialist?
   A. a primary care physician
   B. a cardiologist
   C. a pediatrician
   D. a generalist

10. In the second paragraph, the word *complicated* means _____.
    A. difficult
    B. simple
    C. common
    D. new

HOW DID YOU DO? Count the number of correct answers on your answer sheet. Record this number in the bar graph on the inside back cover.

Describing an Event

A Study the map of Washington, D.C., and read the sentences below. Check (✓) *True* or *False*.

	True	False
1. The Mall is between the Washington Monument and the U.S. Capitol.	☐	☐
2. The White House is directly south of the Washington Monument.	☐	☐
3. To get from the White House to the Capitol building, you can go west on Pennsylvania Avenue.	☐	☐
4. Jefferson Drive runs parallel to Independence Avenue.	☐	☐
5. The National Museum of American History is across the Mall from the Smithsonian Institution.	☐	☐
6. To get from the Capitol building to the Washington Monument, you have to cross 7th St.	☐	☐
7. To get from the Washington Monument to the White House, you have to cross Independence Avenue.	☐	☐
8. To get from the National Air and Space Museum to the National Museum of American History, you can go east on Jefferson Drive and then north on 14th Street.	☐	☐

B Correct the false sentences in Activity A.

_____

_____

_____

_____

_____

C Unscramble the questions. Then match each question to an answer below. Write the letter of the answer on the line.

1. the colors / are / the U.S. / what / flag / of

   _____? _____

2. stars / how many / on / are / the U.S. flag

   _____? _____

3. color / on the U.S. flag / the stars / what / are

   _____? _____

4. what / represent / do / on the flag / the stars

   _____? _____

5. stripes / on the flag / are / how many

   _____? _____

6. do / what / on the flag / the stripes / represent

   _____? _____

7. is / the United States / what / Capitol

   _____? _____

8. the capital / is / what / of / the United States

   _____? _____

Answers

a. the fifty states   c. Washington, D.C.   e. fifty   g. the place where Congress meets

b. thirteen   d. red, white, and blue   f. the original 13 colonies   h. white

D Compare the 2 U.S. flags and write 6 ideas in the Venn Diagram below.

the 1777 flag   both flags   today's flag

Identifying Rights and Responsibilities

A Complete the questions below with the correct form of the word in the box. Then answer the questions.

NOUN	VERB	ADJECTIVE
1. authority	authorize	XXXXX
2. treatment	treat	XXXXX
3. honesty	XXXXX	honest
4. gathering	gather	XXXXX
5. religion	XXXXX	religious
6. belief	believe	believable
7. tolerance	tolerate	tolerant
8. registration	register	XXXXX
9. election	elect	XXXXX
10. respect	respect	respectful

1. In the United States, who has the _____ to make new laws?
   _____

2. What is an example of unfair _____ of an employee by an employer?
   _____

3. How can you tell when someone isn't being _____?
   _____

4. Where in your city do large groups of people sometimes _____?
   _____

5. In which country do people have to accept the _____ beliefs of others?
   _____

6. Do you _____ everything you read in the newspaper?
   _____

7. What kind of behavior is difficult to _____?
   _____

8. Can you_____to vote by mail?
   _____

9. When is the next presidential_____?

_____

10. How can young people show_____to older people?

_____

B Read this information and answer the questions below.

The Bill of Rights

The first ten amendments, or changes, to the U.S. Constitution protect certain freedoms and rights of U.S. citizens by limiting the power of the government. These ten amendments are called The Bill of Rights.

First Amendment Guarantees the rights of freedom of speech, religion, press, peaceable assembly, and to petition the government.

Second Amendment Guarantees the right to bear arms.

Third Amendment Says the government cannot force citizens to house soldiers in their homes during peacetime and without permission.

Fourth Amendment States that the government cannot search or take a person's property without a warrant.

Fifth Amendment Says that a person cannot be tried twice for the same crime or forced to testify against himself or herself.

Sixth Amendment States that people have the right to a fair trial with adequate legal representation.

Seventh Amendment Guarantees a trial by jury in most cases.

Eighth Amendment Prohibits all "cruel and unusual punishment."

Ninth Amendment Says that people have other rights in addition to those listed in the Constitution.

Tenth Amendment States that the powers that the Constitution does not give to the national government belong to the states and to the citizens.

1. Which amendment says you have other rights, in addition to those listed in the Constitution? _____

2. Which amendment allows you to disagree with an action of the government? _____

3. Which amendment prevents the government from telling newspapers what to print?_____

4. Which amendment prevents the government from forcing people to go church? _____

5. Which amendment says the government cannot enter your house without a strong reason? _____

6. Which amendment prevents the government from stopping a protest march? _____

Understanding the US Educational System

A Read these opinions and tell if you agree or disagree. Check (✓) your ideas.

1. In my opinion, all citizens should be required to vote in the presidential election.

   ☐ I think so, too.   ☐ I'm not sure about that.

2. I wish they would raise the speed limit on highways.

   ☐ So do I.   ☐ You do?

3. I think health care should be free.

   ☐ Me too.   ☐ Really? Why is that?

4. I don't like to pay taxes.

   ☐ Neither do I.   ☐ Really? Why not?

5. I don't think children should have to go to school until they are 16.

   ☐ I don't either.   ☐ Really? Why is that?

6. I enjoy reading about history.

   ☐ I do, too.   ☐ You do?

B Complete the conversations so that the people agree.

1. A: I think we should vote in the election tomorrow.

   B: _____

2. A: I don't think people should keep guns at home.

   B: _____

3. A: I think it's important to get a college education.

   B: _____

4. A: I think the voting age should be changed.

   B: _____

5. A: I don't think schools should sell junk food to children.

   B: _____

6. A: I think it's important to study history.

   B: _____

7. A: I prefer coeducational schools.

   B: _____

C Complete the sentences with words from the box.

compulsory	peaceful	encourage
discriminatory	participate	coeducational
responsibility	policy	requirements

1. In some countries, voting is _____ ; you have to do it.

2. The demonstration on the Washington Mall was _____ ; no one caused any problems.

3. Allowing men to vote but not women is _____ .

4. It is the _____ of every citizen to vote in elections.

5. It's important for citizens to _____ in the government. They can do things such as writing letters to their representatives and voting in elections.

6. It is the _____ of the government to encourage people to vote but not to require them to vote.

7. If you don't want your children to attend a _____ school, you will have to send them to a private school.

8. The _____ for entrance into a university vary from one school to another.

9. I think it's important for parents to _____ their children to study hard in school.

D Add the missing verb forms to the chart. Then complete the sentences below with the passive form of the verbs.

SIMPLE FORM	PAST FORM	PAST PARTICIPLE
1. write	wrote	written
2. call		
3. sign		
4. celebrate		
5. elect		
6. build		
7. give		
8. allow		

1. Do you know when the U.S. Constitution _____ ?

2. Can you tell me what the first ten amendments to the Constitution _____ ?

3. Do you know when the U.S. Declaration of Independence _____ ?

4. Do you know when Independence Day _____ in the U.S.?

5. Can you tell me when the first U.S. president _____ ?

6. Do you know when the White House _____ ?

7. Do you remember when women in the U.S. _____ the right to vote for the first time?

8. Do you know when 18-year-olds _____ to vote?

63

Understanding Workers' Rights

A Read the information from a website. Use it to answer the questions below.

⊠ ⊟ ⊞   **www.osha.gov**

U.S. Department of Labor
Occupational Safety & Health Administration
www.osha.gov

Search [   ] GO

Site Index: A B C D E F G H I J K L M N O P Q R S T U V W X Y Z

OSHA Saves Lives

1   "Get out of that trench," OSHA Inspector Robert Dickinson ordered a worker in an unsafe trench by the side of the road near El Paso, Texas. El Paso Assistant Area Director Mario Solano had noticed the trench earlier, and he sent Dickinson and Elia Casillas to check it out. Thirty seconds after the employee got out of the trench, the wall near where he had been standing collapsed. Warning the worker to leave the trench prevented the worker from experiencing a serious injury.

2   On June 10, OSHA compliance officers from the El Paso District Office helped prevent a terrible accident. The two officers were sent to the site of a tower under construction. At the construction site, the two officers found that workers on the tower did not have proper equipment to protect them from an 80 foot fall. The OSHA officers talked with the employer who then instructed the workers to get off the tower. The employer agreed to install a safety system to protect the workers from a fall.

3   In August, two workers were washing windows from a scaffold high up above the ground. Suddenly the scaffold broke, and the two men remained hanging in the air. Luckily the two workers were using the proper safety equipment and they didn't fall to the ground. Soon, the fire department was able to rescue them.

Source: http://www.osha.gov/

1. The information above is from the website of which government agency?

2. In the first story, why did the inspector tell the employee to get out of the trench?

3. In the second story, what did the employer need to do?

4. In the third story, why didn't the workers get hurt?

5. What do these three stories have in common?

6. How is the third story different from the first two?

B Check (✓) the issues you think OSHA is responsible for.

1. Inspecting work sites	☐
2. Discrimination	☐
3. Investigating workplace accidents	☐
4. Retirement plans	☐
5. Proper safety equipment	☐
6. Fair wages	☐
7. Hazards in the workplace	☐
8. Benefits	☐

C Complete the sentences. Use the present perfect passive form of the verb in parentheses.

My brother and I have just opened a new car wash business. We've been very busy. Here's what we've done so far:

Done:

1. Three employees _____ (hire) to wash the cars.

2. Each employee _____ (give) a contract of employment.

3. The employees _____ (give) uniforms and equipment.

4. The car wash equipment _____ (install).

Here are the things we have not done yet:

To Do:

5. The signs _____ (paint / not) yet.

6. The workers _____ (train / not) yet.

7. The flyers _____ (send out / not) yet.

8. The advertisement _____ (write / not) yet.

Reading: Adjusting Your Reading Speed

A Skim the article on page 67 and then complete the sentences below.

1. The title is _____.

2. The headings are _____ and _____.

3. This reading is about _____

4. Does the article look interesting to you? _____.

B Scan the article on page 67 to find the information below.

1. The names of the two parts of the U.S. Congress: _____ _____

2. The number of people in each part of the U.S. Congress: _____ _____

C Read the article and take notes in the chart below.

	The U.S. House of Representatives	The U.S. Senate
1. Total number of people		
2. Number of people per state		
3. Length of term		
4. Responsibilities		

D Think of 3 more things you would like to learn about the U.S. Congress. Write your questions below. Talk about your questions with your classmates.

- _____

- _____

- _____

All About the U.S. Congress

Citizens of the United States vote in free elections to choose people to represent them in the U.S. Congress. Congress has the responsibility of making the laws for our nation. Congress is made up of the House of Representatives and the Senate.

The U.S. House of Representatives

People in each state vote to choose members of the House of Representatives. There are 435 members of the House of Representatives, which is often called "the House." The number of representatives from each state depends on how many people live in that state. States are divided into districts. People living in each district vote for someone to represent their district in the House. Each representative serves for two years, and then people have another chance to vote for them or for a different person to represent them. Representatives can serve in Congress for an unlimited period of time.

The House of Representatives makes laws, but it also has some special responsibilities. Only the House of Representatives can:

• Make laws about taxes.

• Decide if a government official accused of committing a crime against the country should be put on trial in the Senate. This is called "impeachment."

The U.S. Senate

There are 100 Senators in the U.S. Senate. People in each state vote to choose two Senators to represent them in Congress. Senators serve for six years, and then people have another chance to vote for them or for a different person to represent them. Senators can serve in Congress for an unlimited period of time. Senators make laws, but they also have special responsibilities. Only the Senate can:

• Say "yes" or "no" to any agreements the President makes with other countries or organizations of countries. These are called "treaties."

• Say "yes" or "no" to any person the President chooses for high-level jobs, such as Supreme Court judges or officials to run the federal departments, such as the Department of Education or the Department of Health and Human Services.

• Hold a trial for a government official who commits a crime against the United States.

Source: http://uscis.gov/

Writing: Identifying Your Purpose for Writing

A Read each sentence and identify the writer's purpose. Choose from the ideas in the box.

Purposes for Writing

- to give an opinion
- to ask for information
- to ask for help
- to give information
- to persuade
- to invite
- to thank

1. Would you like to come to dinner tonight? _____

2. Can you take this to the post office for me? _____

3. Did you know the schools will be closed tomorrow? _____

4. Do you know the name of a good restaurant? _____

5. I think we need a better public transportation system. _____

6. Please come to the party. A lot of people you know will be there. _____

7. It was very nice of you to help my father get to the store. _____

8. Is there any chance you could take me to school tomorrow? _____

B Read the letter and identify the writer's purpose.

The writer's purpose for writing this letter was to _____

_____

3566 Seventh Street
Rowland Heights, CA 91748
October 10, 2011

Merit Health Insurance Co.
5997 Langdon Road
Lynwood, CA 90262

Dear Sir/Madam:

  This letter is to hereby notify you of my intent to cancel my health policy with Merit Health Insurance, effective November 1, 2011.

Sincerely,

Sarah Miles

Sarah Miles

C Read the letter and answer the questions below.

5449 Orion Road
Paramount, CA 90723
June 16, 2012

Office of Senator Jones
United States Senate
Washington, D.C. 20510

Dear Senator Jones:

 I am writing this letter to voice my support for the ban on ATVs in our parks. I feel strongly that the presence of these vehicles is harmful to the wildlife, water resources, and passive recreation opportunities in our parks. ATV users may deserve a place to use their vehicles, but it should not be in an area where people walk and animals live.

 I urge you to support this ban.

Sincerely,

Jacob Marden
Jacob Marden

---

1. Who is the sender of this letter? _____

2. What salutation did the writer use? _____

3. What is the writer's purpose for writing? _____

_____

4. What does the writer give an opinion about? _____

_____

5. What closing does the writer use? _____

6. Do you think this is an effective letter? Why or why not?

_____

_____

_____

_____

Family: Tenant Rights

A Whose responsibility is it? Check (✓) *Landlord* or *Tenant*.

Whose responsibility is it to _____?

	the landlord	the tenant
1. provide locks and keys for doors	☐	☐
2. get rid of insects, rodents, etc.	☐	☐
3. put trash in trash cans	☐	☐
4. repair the heating system if it breaks	☐	☐
5. provide smoke detectors	☐	☐
6. keep the rental property clean so it doesn't attract insects, rodents, etc.	☐	☐
7. replace batteries in smoke detectors	☐	☐

B Read each person's problem below. Then use the information on page 71 to answer each person's question.

1. I live in a large apartment building, and I often see the landlord go into people's apartments when they are not at home. My neighbor even came home one day when the landlord was in the apartment. He told her he was checking the smoke detectors. Does he really have the right to enter our apartments whenever he wants to? What can we do?
—Stella

Problem: _____

_____

Possible response: _____

_____

2. The shower in my apartment doesn't work properly. I told my landlord about it three weeks ago, but he still hasn't fixed it. I have left him several messages on his answering machine, but he hasn't returned my calls. What should I do?
—Hamid

Problem: _____

_____

Possible response: _____

_____

3. During the summer my landlord sometimes turns the electricity off. He says he is only doing this to make repairs, but I know this isn't true. What can I do?
—Z.B.

Problem: _____

_____

Possible response: _____

_____

4. There's something wrong with the refrigerator in our apartment. We told the landlord about it, and he promised to either fix it or buy us a new one. That was two months ago and still nothing has happened. What can we do?
—Taka

Problem: _____

_____

Possible response: _____

_____

⊠⊟⊞   **IllinoisLawHelp.org**

IllinoisLawHelp.org
Providing Legal Information for Illinois Residents

| | Search |

Choose a topic:

Consumer Law	Education	**Housing**	Senior Citizens
Criminal Law	Family Law	Immigration	Taxes
Disability	Health Care	Public Benefits	Work

Tenant's Rights Fact Sheet

What must a landlord do?

The landlord must:

- keep the home up to local building code;
- keep the home so you can safely live in it;
- give you written notice before ending the lease; and
- not enter the home without telling you in advance, unless it is an emergency.

What must a tenant do?

- keep the home clean;
- not change the home unless the landlord says it is okay;
- pay the rent when it is due;
- obey the lease; and
- tell the landlord about any problems with the home.

How do I get the landlord to make repairs?

You must tell the landlord about the problem. If the landlord does not fix the problem, write the landlord a letter. Send the letter by certified mail. Ask for a return receipt. Keep a copy of the letter.

You may complain to the building department about problems. If the problems are serious, they may condemn the home. Then you would have to move.

If the landlord promises to make repairs, send the landlord a letter saying what the landlord promised to do.

What if the landlord turns the water off?

Water, gas, and electricity are utilities. The landlord may only turn the utilities off to make repairs. The landlord may not turn the utilities off for any other reason. If the landlord does, you can sue the landlord.

Unit 4: Rights and Responsibilities

Community: Voting Rights

A Read questions 1 to 5 below. Then read the FAQs (frequently asked questions) and look for answers to the questions.

1. How old do you have to be to vote in the United States? _____

2. If you move to another town in the same state, do you have to register to vote again? YES NO

3. If November 1st is a Tuesday, what is the date of the presidential election? _____

4. Can I choose where I want to vote? YES NO

5. Which of these people can vote? Check (✓) CAN VOTE or CAN'T VOTE.

1. Mayela
   - is 70 years old
   - is a U.S. citizen
   - moved to Florida last year
   - hasn't registered to vote in Florida
   ☐ CAN VOTE ☐ CAN'T VOTE

2. Fernando
   - his 18th birthday is on 11/1
   - has registered to vote
   - is a U.S. citizen
   - does not have a job
   ☐ CAN VOTE ☐ CAN'T VOTE

3. Lilian
   - is 28 years old
   - just became a U.S. citizen
   - has registered to vote
   - can't speak English
   ☐ CAN VOTE ☐ CAN'T VOTE

FREQUENTLY ASKED QUESTIONS ABOUT VOTING

1) Who can vote in the United States?
In order to vote, you must a) be at least 18 years old by Election Day, b) be a United States citizen, and c) be registered to vote.

2) How do you register to vote?
To *register* means to "sign up." When you register, your name is added to a list of voters. If you move to a new town or city, you must register again to vote. Registration deadlines vary from state to state. In some states, you have to register 30 days before the election. In most places you can register by mail or online.

3) When do you vote?
The election for President is on the Tuesday after the first Monday in November. Other elections are held at different times.

4) Where do you vote?
Your voter registration card tells you where to vote. Most people vote in a place in their neighborhood.

B Answer these questions about the application form below. Circle your answers.

1. In which section should you write the date?	1	4	9
2. In which section should you sign your name?	1	3	9
3. If your home address is the same as your mailing address, which section should you leave blank?	2	3	5
4. Which of these sections can you leave blank?	1	5	9
5. Which section asks you to look at the special instructions for your state?	3	4	7

Voter Registration Application
Before completing this form, review the General, Application, and State specific instructions.

Are you a citizen of the United States of America? ☐ Yes ☐ No	This space for office use only.
Will you be 18 years old on or before election day? ☐ Yes ☐ No	

If you checked "No" in response to either of these questions, do not complete form.
(Please see state-specific instructions for rules regarding eligibility to register prior to age 18.)

1 | (Circle one) Mr. Mrs. Miss Ms. | Last Name | First Name | Middle Name(s) | (Circle one) Jr Sr II III IV

2 | Home address | Apt. or Lot # | City/Town | State | Zip Code

3 | Address Where You Get Your Mail if Different From Above | City/Town | State | Zip Code

4 | Date of Birth ___/___/___ Month Day Year | **5** | Telephone Number (optional) | **6** | ID Number - (See Item 6 in the instructions for your State)

7 | Choice of Party (see item 7 in the instructions for your State) | **8** | Race or Ethnic Group (see item 8 in the instructions for your State)

9 | I have reviewed my state's instructions and I swear/affirm that:
- I am a United States citizen.
- I meet the eligibility requirements of my state and subscribe to any oath required.
- The information I have provided is true to the best of my knowledge under penalty of perjury. If I have provided false information, I may be fined, imprisoned, or (if not a U.S. citizen) deported from or refused entry to the United States.

Please sign full name (or put mark) ▲

Date: ___/___/___ Month Day Year

If you are registering to vote for the first time: please refer to the application instructions for information on submitting copies of valid identification documents with this form.

Practice Test

A   Use the information below to answer the next 5 questions. Use the Answer Sheet.

KNOW YOUR RIGHTS: FEDERAL LAWS PROTECT EMPLOYEES

Several federal laws forbid employers from discriminating against people looking for a job. The United States has laws forbidding discrimination because of:

- Race, color, religion, country of origin, and sex (Civil Rights Act)
- Age (Age Discrimination in Employment Act)
- Disabilities (Americans with Disabilities Act)
- Sex (Equal Pay Act)

For more information about these protections, visit the U.S. Equal Employment Opportunity Commission website at http://www.eeoc.gov or call 1-800-669-4000 or 1-800-669-6820 (for hearing impaired).

Other laws help keep workplaces safe, provide for leave in cases of family or medical emergencies, and provide temporary funds for unemployed workers. Visit the U.S. Department of Labor website at http://www.dol. gov for more information about workers' rights.

ANSWER SHEET

	A	B	C	D
1	Ⓐ	Ⓑ	Ⓒ	Ⓓ
2	Ⓐ	Ⓑ	Ⓒ	Ⓓ
3	Ⓐ	Ⓑ	Ⓒ	Ⓓ
4	Ⓐ	Ⓑ	Ⓒ	Ⓓ
5	Ⓐ	Ⓑ	Ⓒ	Ⓓ
6	Ⓐ	Ⓑ	Ⓒ	Ⓓ
7	Ⓐ	Ⓑ	Ⓒ	Ⓓ
8	Ⓐ	Ⓑ	Ⓒ	Ⓓ
9	Ⓐ	Ⓑ	Ⓒ	Ⓓ
10	Ⓐ	Ⓑ	Ⓒ	Ⓓ

1. Which act protects someone in a wheelchair from discrimination on the job?

   A. Equal Pay Act

   B. Americans with Disabilities Act

   C. Age Discrimination in Employment Act

   D. Civil Rights Act

2. Which act protects you from discrimination because of your religion?

   A. Equal Pay Act

   B. Americans with Disabilities Act

   C. Age Discrimination in Employment Act

   D. Civil Rights Act

3. If you want more information about safety at work, what can you do?

   A. Call 1-800-669-4000.

   B. Call 911.

   C. Visit www.eeoc.gov.

   D. Visit www.dol.gov.

4. Choose the best dictionary meaning for the word *leave* in the article.

   A. go away permanently

   B. to have as a result

   C. a period away from work

   D. permission

5. What does the word *fund* mean in this article?

   A. a large amount of something

   B. money for a specific purpose

   C. a savings account

   D. to sponsor

B Use the information in the graph to answer the next 5 questions. Use the Answer Sheet on page 74.

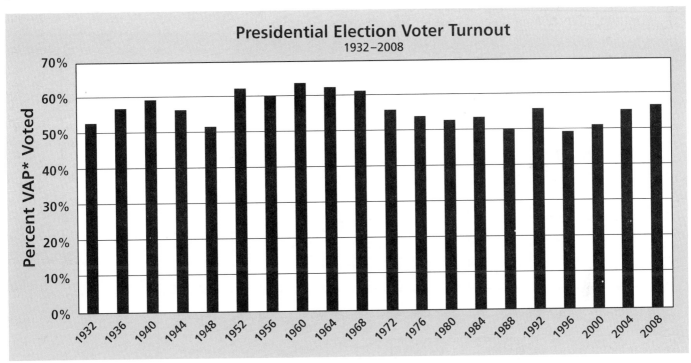

Presidential Election Voter Turnout
1932–2008

*VAP: Voting Age Population

6. In which year was voter turnout the highest?
   A. 1932
   B. 1940
   C. 1960
   D. 1980

7. In which year was voter turnout the lowest?
   A. 1988
   B. 1948
   C. 1996
   D. 2000

8. Which statement is true?
   A. In 1956, 60% of the people didn't vote.
   B. The number of people who have voted has decreased steadily.
   C. More people voted in 1940 than in 1948.
   D. More people vote now than in the past.

9. What information is provided in the graph?
   A. The percent of women who voted.
   B. The percent of people who didn't vote.
   C. The percent of people who voted.
   D. The number of people who voted in each election.

10. In which two years was the voter turnout about the same?
    A. 1948 and 2000
    B. 1932 and 1960
    C. 1988 and 1992
    D. 1948 and 1964

HOW DID YOU DO? Count the number of correct answers on your answer sheet. Record this number in the bar graph on the inside back cover.

Interpreting Advertisements

A Read the advertisements and answer the questions below.

Ad #1

Bob's Furniture

Family Owned and Operated
in Huntington Park since 1961

Bring this ad to get a
10% discount on your
first purchase.

Ad #2

MARDEN'S OF PASADENA

Summer Special
SALE

All sweaters
10% Off

Ad #3

Jimmy's Diner

Breakfast Special*
JUST $2.99
5 Eggs Any Style
Plus Coffee

5495 Ridgely Road
Gardena, CA 90248

*Served between 3 A.M. and 5 A.M. only.

Ad #4

RENT A WRECK
CAR RENTALS

$25.00 A DAY + .05 PER MILE
LAX LOCATION ONLY

You won't find anything cheaper!

Call 555-3499

Ad #5

DOOGAN'S
SALE 50% Off

AYERS
HAIRBRUSHES

Buy two and get the second one
for **50% OFF**

$9.99 Original Price
$4.99 Sale Price

1. If you want to get 10% off a piece of furniture at Bob's, what do you have to do?

_____

2. If you found a $30.00 sweater at Marden's, how much would you pay for it?

_____

3. When can you get the breakfast special at Jimmy's Diner?

_____

4. If you rented a car from Rent a Wreck for three days and you traveled 30 miles each day, how much would you owe?

_____

5. If you bought 2 hairbrushes at Doogan's, how much would you pay?

_____

B Read the information and answer the questions below.

THAT'S MISLEADING!

Advertisers want to get your attention. They want to sell you something or make you do something. Sometimes, however, an advertisement is misleading. That means it gives you information that is not exactly true or is true only under certain conditions. For example, when an advertisement says that a certain food has "reduced fat," it only means that the food has less fat than the original food. The "reduced fat" food may still be high in fat. Saying that a food has "reduced fat" is a little misleading because it makes you think the food has just a little fat.

Have you ever seen one of those "before" and "after" advertisements? They sometimes show a photograph of someone before they lost weight and after they lost weight. These ads can be misleading, too. They don't always show the same person in the "before" photograph and the "after" photograph.

The law protects consumers from some types of misleading advertising. For example, stores are not allowed to use the "bait and switch" sales technique. A store uses the "bait and switch" technique when it advertises a product on sale to get you to go to the store, but it doesn't actually have the product in the store. That's not legal.

---

1. What is the definition of a misleading ad?

   _____

   _____

2. What is the "bait and switch" sales technique?

   _____

   _____

3. If a store advertised something they didn't have, what would you do?

   _____

   _____

4. What is misleading about this bakery ad?

   _____

   _____

TAKE IT OUTSIDE: LOOK IN A NEWSPAPER OR MAGAZINE FOR ADVERTISEMENTS THAT HAVE MISLEADING INFORMATION. BRING YOUR EXAMPLES TO CLASS TO SHARE WITH YOUR CLASSMATES.

Understanding Shopping Terms

A Choose the correct form of the words to complete the questions below. Then answer the questions.

NOUN	VERB	ADJECTIVE
1. refund	refund	refundable
2. product	produce	XXXXX
3. profit	profit	profitable
4. advertisement	advertise	XXXXX
5. selection	select	XXXXX
6. purchase	purchase	XXXXX
7. expiration	expire	XXXXX
8. impulse	XXXXX	impulsive

1. When might you ask for a _____?
   _____

2. What kinds of _____ usually come with a warranty?
   _____

3. What could you buy and then sell at a _____?
   _____

4. In addition to television, where can stores _____?
   _____

5. Which store in your area has the best _____ of fruits and vegetables?
   _____

6. Why might someone return a _____ to a store?
   _____

7. What should you do with unused medicine after its _____ date?
   _____

8. What was the last thing you bought on _____?
   _____

B Complete the conversation. Use the *-ed* or *-ing* forms of the word in parentheses.

A: Jack is _____ (depress) that he didn't get the job he wanted.

B: I know. That's really _____ (disappoint). He was _____ (excite) about the position.

A: He's really _____ (tire), too. The interview process was

_____ (exhaust) for him.

B: I'm _____ (surprise) that he didn't get the job. He's an

_____ (amaze) person.

A: I agree. And the job that he has now is _____ (bore) for him. He needs some

new challenges.

C What could these people do? Write your ideas.

1. Xiao Li bought a sweater for his sister, but the sweater was too small. What do you think Xiao Li should do
    with the sweater?

    _____

    _____

2. Arturo saw an ad for a radio on sale at a nearby store. When he got to the store, however, there weren't
    any radios left. The salesclerk showed Arturo several more radios, but they were much more expensive.
    What could Arturo do?

    _____

    _____

3. Ken is an impulse shopper, especially when he goes shopping for food. He buys more food than his family
    can eat. What could Ken do to stop impulse shopping?

    _____

    _____

4. When Leila went shopping for some new clothes, the salesperson asked if she needed help. What could
    Leila say to the salesperson?

    _____

    _____

5. Cyndi's grandmother needs some new clothes, but it's difficult for her to go shopping. Cyndi offered to go
    shopping for her, but she doesn't want to buy anything her grandmother can't wear. What do you think
    Cyndi should do?

    _____

    _____

Talking to Salespeople

A Number each conversation in order starting with number #1.

Conversation A

_____ Yes, we do—as long as you have another form of identification.

_____ Yes, I'd like to pay for these.

_____ Yes. That would be fine.

_____ Okay. How would you like to pay for them?

___1___ Can I help you?

_____ Will a driver's license do?

_____ Do you take credit cards?

Conversation B

_____ Do you have your receipt?

___1___ Can I help you?

_____ Yes, I do. Here it is.

_____ I'd rather get cash back.

_____ Okay. I can give you store credit for that amount.

_____ Can I speak to the manager, please?

_____ Yes, of course.

_____ Yes, I'd like to return this.

_____ I'm sorry, but we only give store credit.

Conversation C

_____ Yes, of course. They come with a two-year warranty.

___1___ Can I help you?

_____ That's correct. But you can also buy an extended warranty.

_____ Yes, can you tell me what the warranty is on the television sets?

_____ But it's only $5 a month. Really, it's a very good deal.

_____ Did you say two years?

_____ No thank you. I'll take the television set, but I'm not interested in an extended warranty.

_____ No, thank you. I'm not interested in an extended warranty.

Conversation D

_____ And how would you like to pay for that?

_____ Yes, you have 30 days to return something.

_____ Yes, of course. But be sure to bring the receipt with you.

___1___ Can I help you?

_____ Is there a time limit?

_____ Yes. Can I bring this back if it doesn't fit my husband?

_____ That's good. I'll take this, then.

_____ Yes, of course. You can make an exchange or a return. Be sure to bring the receipt with you.

_____ By cash.

B Complete these sentences.

1. If a store accepts only cash or credit card, you cannot pay by _____

2. If something is nonreturnable, you can't _____

3. If you lose the receipt for something you purchased, you can't _____

4. If a salesperson tries to pressure you into buying something, you can _____

5. If something comes with a warranty, you can _____

6. If you buy things in bulk, you can _____

7. If something is advertised "on sale" but is out of stock, you can _____

8. If you can't find something in a store, you should _____

C Add the correct tag to each statement on the right. Write the tag on the line.

1. He didn't like it, _____?   a. can she

2. That was a profitable business, _____?   b. isn't it

3. He speaks Spanish very well, _____?   c. was it

4. That's the end of the movie, _____?   d. do they

5. Shoes cost a lot, _____?   e. is it

6. It wasn't very cold yesterday, _____?   f. did he

7. She can't sing very well, _____?   g. didn't he

8. Clothes from thrift stores don't cost a lot, _____?   h. wasn't it

9. That dress isn't very pretty, _____?   i. don't they

10. He certainly left in a hurry, _____?   j. doesn't he

D Agree or disagree with each tag question below.

1. A: Shakespeare was a great writer, wasn't he?

   B: _____

2. A: This is great music, isn't it?

   B: _____

3. A: Mexican food is delicious, isn't it?

   B: _____

4. A: It's not easy to learn a new language, is it?

   B: _____

5. A: Email is really fast, isn't it?

   B: _____

Using Resources to Find Housing

A Write the abbreviation for each term.

1. bedroom _____

2. washer and dryer _____

3. security deposit _____

4. hookup _____

5. utilities _____

B Read this information and answer the questions on page 83.

Houses for Rent

(A) 2BR, W/D, 2 BA, no pets, no smokers, $1,200/mo. 555-0983

(B) 3 BR house, W/D included. $900/mo. 555-6574

(C) Lowell Heights 2 BR, 2 BA. $1000/mo. + sec. dep. Call Pam 555-1134

(D) PIKE HILL 2BR house, W/D, new refrigerator, small backyard. $1,250/mo + utils. 555-2251

(E) OLD TOWN New 2 BR, 2 baths, pool, pets ok. $1100/mo. Call Alan 555-4378

(F) 3 BR home w/ porch and small yard. No pets. $1100. Call Sue 555-2211

(G) HYDE VALLEY 4 BR, 2.5 BA, $1350/mo. Call after 6 p.m. 555-0912

Condominium Rentals

(H) 1-BR condo, central air. $1275/mo. Call Tammy 555-3343

(I) 2 BR, includes utils. Cats OK. No dogs. $900/mo. + sec. dep. Call Lulu 555-8810

(J) OLD TOWN Lg 1BR, parking, W/D hkup, a/c, utils included. $850/mo. 555-5295

Furnished Apartments

(K) DOWNTOWN 2 BR, 1 BA. a/c, prkg & utils included, no smokers/pets. $950/mo. 555-4725

(L) 1BR/1BA, small LR, big kitchen, prkg, nice area, sec. dep, $200/wk. 555-3854

KEY
BR = bedroom(s)
sec dep = security deposit
W/D = washer and dryer
hkup = hookup
utils = utilities
a/c = air conditioning
ht = heat
hw = hot water
prkg = parking

Unfurnished Apartments

(M) PIKE HILL Lg 2 BR, laundry, prking, utils included, small yard, no pets/smokers, $990/mo. Call 555-2864

(N) Hyde Valley 2 BR/2 BA. safe neighborhood, new kitchen, prking, no utils, $950/mo. 555-0115

(O) LOWELL HEIGHTS Lg 1 BR, 1 BA, gar, backyard, small dog ok. $800/mo. + sec. dep. 555-6728

(P) PIKE HILL 1 BR/1 BA, new refrigerator/stove, no smokers/pets, $1,050/mo. + sec. dep. 555-3399

(Q) 2BR, nice neighborhood, no pets, a/c, utils included. $800/mo. + sec. dep. Call Linda after 5 p.m. 555-2745

C Read the description of each person or couple. Match each one to an apartment, a condominium, or a house ad on page 82. Write the letter of the ad in the chart.

Ads	People
_____	1. **Mike** and **Carrie** have two children, a boy and a girl. They are looking for a large place with at least two bathrooms. Carrie works at home, so she needs an office.
_____	2. **Cathy** wants to live by herself. She can pay up to $875 a month for rent. She prefers a condominium or apartment because she doesn't have time to take care of a yard. She has a dog and needs a place to park her car.
_____	3. **Pedro** and **Marta** have one daughter. They don't smoke and they don't have any pets. They want a place with parking and paid utilities. They don't want to live downtown. They can pay up to $1,000 a month for rent.
_____	4. **Ben** is looking for a large place. His friends and family often visit, so he needs a couple of extra bedrooms. He wants a place with a washer and dryer. He can afford to pay $1,150 a month for rent.
_____	5. **Elaine** wants to pay between $600 and $900 a month. She wants an extra bedroom to use as an office. She has a cat.

D Complete the conversation with the sentences in the box.

How much is the security deposit?	Is there a garage?
Is it still available?	Is there a laundry room in the building?
Can I come and see the apartment?	Are pets allowed?

Landlord: Hello.

Elaine: Hello, I'm calling about the apartment for rent. _____

Landlord: Yes, it is. Do you have any questions about it?

Elaine: Yes, I have a few questions. I have a cat. _____

Landlord: Yes, I allow cats, but not dogs.

Elaine: Great. _____

Landlord: No, but there are washer and dryer hookups in the apartment.

Elaine: Oh, that's good. _____

Landlord: No, there isn't. There's only street parking.

Elaine: OK. _____

Landlord: It's $500.

Elaine: _____

Landlord: Sure, you can come by this Saturday. I'm showing it from 8:00 A.M. to noon.

Reading: Using a Dictionary

A Read the dictionary entries. Answer the questions.

> **sell** /*v*. (past tense and past participle **sold**) **1**. [I,T] to give something to someone in exchange for money **(ant.)** buy: *I sold him my car for $4,000*. **2**. to offer something for people to buy: *Bananas sell for about $.69 a pound*. **3**. to make someone want to buy something: *Advertisers use children and animals to sell products*. **4**. to try to make someone accept a new plan, idea, etc.: *The president tried to sell his new health policy to the public*.
>
> **sell** sth **off** *phr v*. to sell something, especially cheaply, because you need the money or want to get rid of it: *The store is selling off all its merchandise*.
>
> **sell out** *phr v*. **1**. to sell all of something so that there is nothing left: *The concert is sold out*. **2**. (informal) to do something that is against your beliefs or principles, in order to get power or money: *The senator has sold out to please the tobacco lobby*.

1. What is the most common meaning of *sell*?

   _____

2. What is the past participle of sell?

   _____

3. What does the abbreviation *sth* mean?

   _____

4. What does the abbreviation *phr v.* mean?

   _____

5. Would you use the verb *sell out* in a formal writing assignment?

   _____

6. What is the antonym of *sell*?

   _____

7. When would you *sell off* your books?

   _____

B Read the sentences. Choose the correct definition for the word *check* in each context. Circle 1, 2, 3 or 4.

> **check** /*n*. **1**. one of a set of printed pieces of paper that you can sign and use to pay for things: *Can I pay by check?* **2**. a careful look at or test of something, to see if it is correct, in good condition: *We need to do a check of the security system*. **3**. something that controls something else and stops it from increasing: *This vaccine should put a check on the spread of the disease*. **4**. a list you are given in a restaurant showing how much you must pay. (syn.) bill, tab: *Can I have the check, please?*

1. She asked for the **check**.   1   2   3   4
2. You should do a **check** of the house before we leave.   1   2   3   4
3. Do you want to pay by **check** or by credit card?   1   2   3   4
4. They hired a guard to put a **check** on shoplifting.   1   2   3   4
5. Before the concert, they did a sound **check**.   1   2   3   4

C Read the dictionary entries and the usage note. Answer the questions.

> **start** / v. **1.** [I,T] to begin doing something: *It **started** to rain.* **2.** [I, T] to begin happening: *The class **starts** in five minutes.* **3.** [T] also **start up** to begin a new business or business activity: *He left the company to **start** a business on his own.* **4.** [I] also **start off/out** to begin a trip: *We should **start** early to get there on time.* **5.** [I, T] also **start up** begin to work: *I can't get the engine to **start**.*
>
> **USAGE NOTE:** **Start** and **begin** usually mean the same thing, but **start** has several meanings for which you cannot use **begin**.
>
> Use **start** in order to talk about making a machine work: *I couldn't start the car this morning.*
>
> Use **start** in order to talk about making something begin to exist: *Starting a new business is hard work.*

1. What is another way to say: *Jack started the lawn mower.* _____

_____

2. What is the purpose of the usage note? _____

_____

3. Is the usage note helpful to you? Why or why not? _____

_____

D Read the sentences and choose the correct definition for the word *start* in each context. Circle 1, 2, 3, 4, or 5.

1. Have you **started** making dinner yet?   1   2   3   4   5
2. When does the new semester **start**?   1   2   3   4   5
3. Before you **start** a restaurant, you should get to know   1   2   3   4   5
   the neighborhood.
4. Can you **start** this DVD for me?   1   2   3   4   5
5. The race **starts** in ten minutes.   1   2   3   4   5

Writing: Writing a Letter of Complaint

A Give a reason to complete each sentence below.

1. I want to return this television set because _____

2. I was unhappy with the service at your store because _____

3. The main reason I am returning this coat is that _____

4. I've decided to return this computer because _____

5. I'd like to return this coffee maker; it _____

B Read the conversation between Cathy and Shirin. Then complete the conversation between Cathy and Tom. Use reported speech.

Cathy: Hi, Shirin. What are you doing?

Shirin: I'm looking for the phone number for this mail order company.

Cathy: Why?

Shirin: I ordered three things, and there's something wrong with all of them.

Cathy: Really?

Shirin: Yeah, the sweater is blue instead of red, the shirt doesn't fit me, and I think the zipper on the jacket is broken.

Cathy: How annoying! What are you going to do?

Shirin: I'm going to call and complain.

Cathy: I just talked to Shirin.

Tom: Oh, what was she doing?

Cathy: She said she _____ for the phone number
                                    (1)
of a mail order company because she ordered three things, and

they were all wrong.

Tom: What do you mean?

Cathy: She told me that the sweater _____ the wrong color, the shirt _____
                                              (2)   (3)
her, and she _____ that the zipper on the jacket _____ broken.
                    (4)   (5)

Tom: Oh, no. What's she going to do?

Cathy: She said she _____ to call and complain.
                            (6)

C Complete the return form below. Use information from the story in Activity B.

DARBY'S RETURN/EXCHANGE

GUARANTEED 100%
NO QUESTIONS. NO EXCEPTIONS.

1 Name: Shirin Hamadi

Phone: (562) 555-4993

Street	City	State	Zip
543 Bennett St. Apt. 4A	Long Beach	CA	90806

2 DESCRIBE REASON(S) Please describe the problem(s) as specifically as possible so that we can improve our products for you. Your input here makes a big difference.

_____

_____

_____

REASON CODES Use one code to explain why you are returning item(s). Please describe the problem(s) in detail above.

APPAREL	SERVICE	QUALITY	SATISFACTION
14 Too small	18 Wrong item sent	22 Defective	26 Did not like color
15 Too short	19 Duplicate ship	23 Didn't like fabric	27 Did not like style
16 Too large	20 Damaged	24 Shrunk	28 Item not as described
17 Too long	21 Arrived too late	25 Poor quality	29 Item not as pictured

3 ITEMS YOU ARE RETURNING Please list any items that you are returning. Be sure to include one reason code for each item from the "Reason Codes" in Section 2.

Reason Code	Qty.	Item #	Description	Size	Color	Price
		075	sweater	M		$28.00
		862	jacket	M		$46.00
		407	shirt	M		$16.50

Community: Consumer Rights

A Read the definitions. Then circle the correct adjective in each sentence.

> **cracked:** broken, but not separated into two or more pieces
> **defective:** not made correctly or not working correctly
> **missing:** not present; absent
> **scratched:** having a thin cut or mark
> **stained:** having a spot that's difficult to clean, usually made from a liquid
> **torn:** having a tear or a hole (paper or fabric)

1. My sunglasses are (stained / scratched). There's a line in the middle of the lens.

2. This jacket is (defective / torn). There's a hole in the front.

3. This toaster doesn't work. It's (stained / defective).

4. The coffee pot that I bought is (cracked / torn). Maybe it got damaged in shipping. It wasn't wrapped very well.

5. This sweater is (defective / stained). It looks like someone spilled coffee on it.

6. I couldn't put this table together. Some parts are (missing / scratched).

B Practice the conversation with a partner. Then practice again. Replace the underlined words with your own ideas.

A: Can I help you?

B: Yes, I'd like to return <u>this jacket</u>.

A: Do you have your receipt? You'll need that for a full refund.

B: Yes, I do. Here it is.

A: Thank you. Is there something wrong with <u>the jacket</u>?

B: <u>It's torn. There's a hole in the back</u>.

A: I see. Would you like to exchange it for another one?

B: <u>No</u>, I'd like a store credit, please.

CONVERSATION STRATEGY

Returning an Item to a Store

Use these words to say what you want when you return something to a store.

exchange = to replace one item with a different item

a store credit = credit that you can use to buy something from the same store

refund = a return of the money that you spent

C Read the paragraph below. Then answer the questions.

Postal Services

When you want to be sure that something you send arrives at its destination safely, you have a couple of choices. You can use **certified mail**, and the post office will send you a receipt showing when the letter or package was mailed. You can use the number on the receipt to check the delivery online. With certified mail, you can also pay extra to get a **return receipt**. The return receipt contains the signature of the person who received the letter or package. The second choice is **registered mail**. It is the most secure mailing method that the post office provides. When you use registered mail, the post office keeps track of your letter or package until it is delivered. You can buy up to $25,000 of **insurance** for your letter or package, and you can check the time of delivery online or by telephone.

1. What service should you ask for if you want to receive a receipt with the signature of the person who you sent a letter or package to? _____

2. What choice should you ask for if you want to receive a receipt that shows only when your letter or package was mailed? _____

3. What should you use if you want to buy insurance for a letter or package? _____

4. How much insurance can you buy for your letter or package? _____

5. What is the most secure way of sending mail through the post office? _____

D Practice the conversation with a partner. Then pratice again. Replace the underlined words with your own ideas.

A: Can I help you?

B: Yes, I'd like to send this letter to <u>New York</u> by <u>certified mail</u>. How much will that cost?*

A: Let's see. That will be <u>$.44 for the letter and $2.65 for certified mail</u>. Would you like a return receipt?

B: <u>Yes, please</u>.

A: OK. That's an additional $2.15. Would you like to buy insurance for the letter?

B: <u>No, thank you</u>.

A: OK. Have you filled out the form?

B: Yes, here it is.

A: Thank you. That will be <u>$5.24</u>. Would you like a receipt?

B: Yes, please.

> ***Useful Expressions**
>
> to ask about the total price
> How much will that cost?
> How much will that be?
> What's the charge for that?

Community: Consumer Resources

A Use the list of Resources for Consumers below to answer these questions.

1. Which resource provides information about different types of insurance? _____

2. Which 3 resources are U.S. federal government agencies? _____ _____

   _____

3. Which federal agency would handle a complaint about false advertising? _____

4. What does the acronym HUD stand for? _____

5. How could you file a complaint with the FTC? _____

6. How can you get in touch with the ACLU? _____

Resources for Consumers

Consumers can get help from federal and state government agencies and from many consumer advocacy groups. Here are just a few of the available resources:

The American Civil Liberties Union (ACLU)

The American Civil Liberties Union focuses on issues affecting individual freedom. To contact them, call a local ACLU office listed in your telephone directory.

Attorneys General

If you have a consumer issue involving the laws of your state, contact your state attorney general.

Better Business Bureaus (BBB)

The Council of Better Business Bureaus has more than 100 local offices nationwide. Check out a business or find out about the dispute resolution program. Look in your telephone book for the nearest BBB.

The Federal Communications Commission (FCC)

The Federal Communications Commission oversees interstate and international communications by radio, television, wire, satellite, and cable. To make a complaint or obtain information, call 888-CALL-FCC.

The Federal Trade Commission (FTC)

The Federal Trade Commission is responsible for enforcing numerous consumer protection laws focusing on deceptive and unfair trade practices.

To file a complaint or obtain information, call 877-FTC-HELP.

The U.S. Department of Housing and Urban Development (HUD)

The U.S. Department of Housing and Urban Development is responsible for handling complaints regarding housing discrimination, manufactured housing, and land sales.

INSURE.COM

This website provides consumer information and resources on life, health, car, and home insurance.

NOLO.COM

Nolo provides legal information for consumers on many different consumer topics; 800-728-3555.

Public Citizen

Founded by Ralph Nader, Public Citizen is a consumer advocacy organization that promotes consumer interest in energy, environment, trade, health, and government issues.

From "Resources for Consumers" from *Understanding Consumer Rights* by Nicolette Parsi and Marc Robinson, New York: Dorling Kindersley, 2000.

B Read about each person below and answer the questions.

1. Sylvia found an apartment she liked, but as soon as the owner of the building learned that she had young children, he said the apartment was no longer available. Which of the resources on page 90 could she get help from? _____

2. James found a roofing company to put a new roof on his house, but he doesn't know if it does good work. Which of the resources on page 90 could he use to get information about the roofing company? _____

3. Fatima bought a toaster oven from a hardware store in her town. When she got home, she found that it didn't work. Now the store refuses to take it back. Which of the resources on page 90 could she get help from? _____

4. Bob just bought a used car from a used car dealer. The dealer tells him he doesn't need a lot of insurance for the car, but Bob is not sure. Which of the resources on page 90 could he get help from? _____

C Choose the correct form of the words to complete the sentences.

VERB	NOUN
1. complain	complaint
2. protect	protection
3. discriminate	discrimination
4. inform	information
5. organize	organization
6. resolve	resolution

1. You have the right to _____ if you buy something that doesn't work. You can send a letter of _____ to the FTC.

2. The goal of the ACLU is to _____ the freedom of individuals.

3. _____ because of your age is illegal in the U.S.

4. NOLO can _____ you about many different legal issues.

5. The BBB is an _____ that gives useful information about businesses in your area.

6. Most businesses want to _____ problems with their customers.

....

TAKE IT OUTSIDE: TALK TO SEVERAL PEOPLE YOU KNOW. ASK THEM THE QUESTIONS BELOW.

1. Have you ever had a problem with a store or a business?

2. What was the problem?

3. What did you do?

Practice Test

A Read the dictionary entry below to answer the next 6 questions. Use the answer sheet.

(a) (b) (c) (d)

trick / trɪk / *n.*   **1.** something you do to deceive or tease someone: *When we were young, my brother liked to* (e) *hide my book bag before school. It was his favorite trick.* **2.** a clever way to do something: *What's the trick to saving* (g) (f) *money on groceries?* **3.** an act that seems like magic, and which is done to entertain people: *The magician did a trick with a rabbit and a hat.*

(h)

—*adj.* a trick question: a question that seems easy to answer, but is actually hard to answer: *The interviewer asked me a lot of trick questions. I think he was trying to confuse me.*

(i)   (j)   (k)   (l)

tricky / trɪki / *adj.* —ier, —iest difficult or full of problems, (syn.) complex, thorny: *Driving around in the dark without a map was tricky, but we finally found Tom's house.*

---

1. Which part of the dictionary entry tells you how to pronounce "trick"?
   A. a
   B. b
   C. c
   D. d

2. Which part of the dictionary entry tells you the part of speech of "trick"?
   A. a
   B. c
   C. d
   D. j

3. Where is a synonym for "tricky"?
   A. i
   B. h
   C. l
   D. k

4. Which part of the dictionary entry tells you the comparative and superlative forms of "tricky"?
   A. d
   B. e
   C. j
   D. k

5. Which part of the dictionary shows you the definition for the adjective "trick"?
   A. d
   B. f
   C. h
   D. k

6. Which definition of "trick" best fits the usage in this sentence? *The trick to opening the door is to turn the key slowly.*
   A. d
   B. e
   C. f
   D. k

ANSWER SHEET			
1	(A)	(B)	(C)	(D)
2	(A)	(B)	(C)	(D)
3	(A)	(B)	(C)	(D)
4	(A)	(B)	(C)	(D)
5	(A)	(B)	(C)	(D)
6	(A)	(B)	(C)	(D)
7	(A)	(B)	(C)	(D)
8	(A)	(B)	(C)	(D)
9	(A)	(B)	(C)	(D)
10	(A)	(B)	(C)	(D)

B Use the information below to answer the next 4 questions. Use the Answer Sheet on page 92.

Examples of Misleading Ads for Telephone Service

Telephone Company A advertised long-distance calls for only 5 cents per minute. However, the company did not say clearly in its ads that there was also a $7.95 monthly fee.

Telephone Company B advertised long-distance calls for only 5 cents per minute. However, the company didn't say that there was a minimum charge of $1 for every call, even if it was a short call.

---

7. If you had your telephone service with Company A and you used the phone for only one minute during the month, how much would you pay?

   A. 7 cents
   B. 70 cents
   C. $7.95
   D. $8.00

8. If you had your telephone service with Company A and you used the phone for 300 minutes in one month, how much would you pay?

   A. $157.95
   B. $22.95
   C. $150.00
   D. $15.00

9. If you had your telephone service with Company B and you used the phone for only one minute during the month, how much would you pay?

   A. 5 cents
   B. $1.00
   C. $1.05
   D. $100.00

10. If you had your telephone service with Company B, which statement below would be true?

   A. A five-minute call is cheaper than a ten-minute call.
   B. A twenty-minute call is as expensive as a thirty-minute call.
   C. A one-minute call and a twenty-minute call cost the same.
   D. A five-minute call costs 25 cents.

HOW DID YOU DO? Count the number of correct answers on your answer sheet. Record this number in the bar graph on the inside back cover.

Describing a Court of Law

A Look at the photo below. Identify the people. Use the words in the box.

jury   witness   judge   attorney   ~~court reporter~~

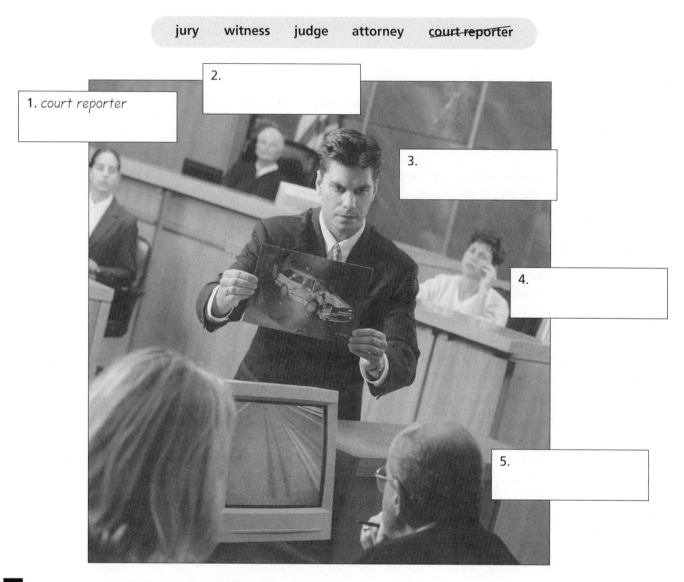

1. court reporter

2.

3.

4.

5.

B Look at the photo above. Check (✓) *True* or *False*.

	True	False
1. The witness is a man.	☐	☐
2. The attorney is showing a photo of tire marks to the judge.	☐	☐
3. Jury members can see information on computers.	☐	☐
4. This case involves battery and disturbing the peace.	☐	☐
5. The testimony probably involves a traffic accident.	☐	☐

C Read the newspaper article about the trial. Answer the questions below in complete sentences.

Harris Trial in Second Day
Witness: "I was terrified!"

The trial of James Harris continued today as jurors heard witness testimony about the hit-and-run accident.

Lynn Rogers described how Harris ran a red light and hit the passenger side of her car, then drove off into busy commuter traffic.

"I was terrified," Rogers testified. "I'm just so thankful that my family wasn't in the car when he hit me."

Rogers told the packed courtroom that seconds after she was hit, she saw Harris crash into another vehicle a couple hundred yards away.

"It was horrible," Rogers said. "I thought someone might have been hurt, so I immediately called 911." The police and paramedics arrived quickly and took Harris into custody, after treating him for minor injuries.

Jurors appeared visibly upset as they viewed photos of the crash scene.

---

1. What is the name of the defendant?

   _____

2. Who is the witness?

   _____

3. Why is the defendant on trial?

   _____

D Read the situations. Write advice for each person. Use the words in parentheses.

1. I need to get a new computer for school.

   (should) _____

2. I want to take an accounting class at the college, but I don't have enough money.

   (ought to) _____

3. I forgot to do my homework.

   (should / shouldn't) _____

4. I got a summons for jury duty, but I am going on vacation.

   (could) _____

5. I have jury duty, but I lost my summons, and I don't know where the courthouse is.

   (ought to) _____

Identifying Infractions and Crimes

A   Write the correct form of the words to complete the sentences.

1. If you _____ (violation / violate) a law, you might be arrested.

2. For serious crimes, you may face _____ (imprisonment / imprison) of up to 20 years.

3. The _____ (punishment / punish) for misdemeanors is less than one year in prison.

4. If you are _____ (conviction / convicted) of a crime, you will have a criminal record.

5. You should make a report to the police if you are the victim of a _____. (robbery / rob)

6. If someone is killed during the _____ (commission / commit) of a felony, the criminal will face additional charges.

7. He _____ (offense / offended) the police officer, and so he was arrested.

8. The jury voted to _____ (conviction / convict) the defendant on a misdemeanor rather than a felony.

9. _____ (burglary / burglarize) is a crime against property, rather than directly against a person.

10. Writing on walls is a type of _____. (vandalism / vandalize)

B   Write a sentence about each photo using a word from Activity A.

1.

2.

1. _____

2. _____

C Complete the sentences. Use *should have*, *shouldn't have* and the verb in parentheses.

1. Daniel had an accident today. He _____ (look) to his left before going through the intersection.

2. The Santos' house was burglarized last night. They _____ (leave) their windows open.

3. Marcy spent all her savings on new clothes. Now she doesn't have enough money to get her car fixed. Marcy _____ (save) some money for an emergency.

D Complete the sentences. Use *should have* or *shouldn't have* and a verb.

1. Robert got a ticket for running through a red light. He _____ at the light.

2. Paula was in a hurry and didn't put her seat belt on. Now she has a traffic infraction. She _____ before she started driving.

3. Jack and Jill both failed their math class because they thought they understood all the material. They _____ before the final exam.

4. Ricardo forgot to set his alarm and was late for work again. His boss gave him another warning. Ricardo _____ .

5. Asha was texting a friend on her cell phone, and she ran into the sidewalk. She _____ while she was driving.

E Answer each question with a complete sentence. Use *could have* or *must have*.

1. Someone stole the radio from Wei's car. What could she have done to prevent this?

_____

_____

2. The football team did not get to the playoffs this year because they weren't prepared for the competition. What could the team have done to be better prepared?

_____

_____

3. John got lost on his way to the restaurant. What could he have done to prevent this?

_____

_____

4. Nancy didn't show up for the test. What could have happened to her?

_____

_____

5. Bob has been in prison for five years. What kind of illegal action must he have committed?

_____

_____

Interpreting Permit and License Requirements

A Unscramble the words to write sentences.

1. the Marriage License Division / reached / have / you

   _____

2. required / premarital / are / physicals / not

   _____

3. it is issued / valid / is / for 60 days thereafter / the marriage license / on the day / and

   _____

   _____

4. $50 / the cost / in cash / is

   _____

5. processed / applications / are / from 8:30 to 4:00

   _____

6. to complete / take / 45 minutes / approximately / will / the application process

   _____

   _____

7. on the application / your social security number / have / must / you

   _____

8. bring / your date of birth / you must / a valid driver's license / or photo ID / with

   _____

B Complete the telephone conversation with information from Activity A.

1. A. Do I need to have a physical exam before I can get a marriage license?

   B. _____

2. A. How long will it take to get the license?

   B. _____

3. A. So do you think I will be finished in half an hour?

   B. _____

4. A: What are your hours?

   B. _____

5. A. Did you say it would cost $75?

   B. _____

6. A. I don't have a driver's license. What should I do?

   B. _____

C Paraphrase the following statements.

1. If you are between the ages of 18 and 21, you must present a valid driver's license or photo ID, and a certified birth certificate.

   _____

   _____

2. You must complete driver's education before you can take the test to get a learner's permit.

   _____

   _____

3. A permit is required to deposit garbage at the county dump site.

   _____

   _____

4. Recyclables, such as glass bottles and aluminum containers, may be brought in to the recycling center without a permit as long as they are kept separate from trash.

   _____

   _____

   _____

Participating in Your Community

A What do you remember about the Neighborhood Watch brochure? Read each statement and check *True* or *False*.

		True	False
1.	Neighborhood Watch groups sometimes invite speakers to talk about safety and crime.	☐	☐
2.	These groups hire police officers to drive through the neighborhood and look for suspicious behavior.	☐	☐
3.	Neighborhood Watch groups are started by concerned citizens.	☐	☐
4.	Members of the group are supposed to look out for strange cars driving slowly through the neighborhood.	☐	☐
5.	If members notice something suspicious, they're supposed to call the leader of the group.	☐	☐

B Read the information and answer the questions on page 101.

Making Changes

Neighborhood Watch is an organization of citizens in a neighborhood. The members of a Neighborhood Watch program work with the police to protect their community. Neighborhood Watch members watch for unusual activity in their neighborhood and report it to the police.

It's a story of hard work and pride. In 1975, Trong Nguyen arrived in Chicago from Vietnam. He and his family were fleeing the last days of war.

But the "Uptown" area the refugees moved into seemed like another war zone. The streets were filled with muggers, drug addicts, and other dangerous people. It was not a good place for families with children.

But people like Trong Nguyen were determined to save the neighborhood. They worked with police and other community leaders. Groups were formed to watch for trouble. Before long, much of the crime stopped.

Meanwhile, Trong opened a small restaurant. Other people from Laos, Cambodia, and Vietnam started businesses in stores that had been empty. Soon, the addicts and gangs disappeared.

Today, Chicago's "Uptown" is no longer a dangerous, run-down area, thanks to Trong and others. People from all over the city come to visit its stores and restaurants. It's a special place.

Source: From "Making Changes," *U.S. Express*, October 21, 1988, Vol 1, No. 3, Scholastic, Inc.

Answer the questions with complete sentences.

1. When did Trong arrive in Chicago?

   _____

2. Why wasn't Trong's neighborhood in Chicago a good place to live?

   _____

3. What did Trong do to change his neighborhood?

   _____

4. What happened after Trong took action to save his neighborhood?

   _____

5. What is Trong's neighborhood like now?

   _____

C Use the cues to write sentences with the correct form of *be* and (*not*) *supposed to.*

1. A: _____ I _____ wait here for the blood test?

   B: No, you _____ _____ wait in the room down the hall.

2. A: When _____ we _____ be at the courthouse?

   B: We _____ _____ be there at 9:00. Hurry! It's already 8:30.

3. A: You _____ _____ exercise right after you eat. It can make you sick.

   B: How long _____ you _____ wait after you eat?

4. A: Where were you? You _____ - _____ be at my house at 7:00. I had to
   take a taxi here.

   B: Oh, no! _____ I _____ pick you up? I'm sorry. I forgot.

D Complete the questions with the verbs in parentheses. Then write answers to the questions. Use
supposed to in your questions and answers.

1. Q: What kinds of things are Community Watch members _____ (look) for in their
   neighborhoods?

   A: _____

2. Q: If you see thieves in your neighborhood, _____ you _____
   (stop) them?

   A: _____

3. Q: What _____ (do) if you see someone taking things from your neighbor's
   house?

   A: _____

Reading: Recognizing Cause and Effect

A Read the following sentences. Write the causes and effects on the lines.

1. He had to go to court because he got three traffic tickets.

   Cause: _____

   Effect: _____

2. The Republicans lost seats in the election. As a result, the Democrats took control of the Senate.

   Cause: _____

   Effect: _____

3. Due to the rise in gas prices, bus ridership increased dramatically.

   Cause: _____

   Effect: _____

4. Because of the dramatic decrease in the murder rate, the county saved $20,000 in the cost of prosecution last year.

   Cause: _____

   Effect: _____

5. The people in my neighborhood organized a community watch program. Consequently, crime in our neighborhood has gone down.

   Cause: _____

   Effect: _____

B Combine the following sentences. Use one of the words or phrases in the box to show the cause/effect relationship.

because	since	if
as a result	for this reason	consequently

1. I watch the news every night. I'm very well-informed.

   _____

2. The defendant was sentenced to five years in prison. He was found guilty.

   _____

3. She missed three days of work. She got a terrible flu.

   _____

C Read the information and find three cause/effect relationships. Write them in the chart below.

Franklin Delano Roosevelt was the 32nd president of the United States. He was also the only president to be elected four times, serving from 1933 until his death on April 12, 1945. When he was 39, Roosevelt contracted polio and had difficulty walking for the rest of his life.

At the time he was elected, the United States was in a terrible economic depression. Roosevelt quickly proposed a sweeping program, the New Deal, that would help businesses economically and provide relief to thousands of unemployed people. It also set up social safety nets, such as Social Security, that are still in effect today.

When the Japanese attacked Pearl Harbor, the United States entered into World War II. Roosevelt led the country through most of the war, dying just before the war ended. He is remembered for his leadership during the devastating depression and war.

Cause	Effect
1.	
2.	
3.	

D Answer the questions in complete sentences.

1. Why did Roosevelt have to use a wheelchair?

_____

2. Why did he introduce the policies and programs of the New Deal?

_____

3. Why do you think Roosevelt is one of the most well-known American presidents?

_____

E Summarize the article.

_____

_____

_____

_____

_____

Writing: Using a Graphic Organizer

A Use the diagrams to organize your answers to the cause/effect questions below. Then write a paragraph to answer each question.

1. What are three causes of homelessness?

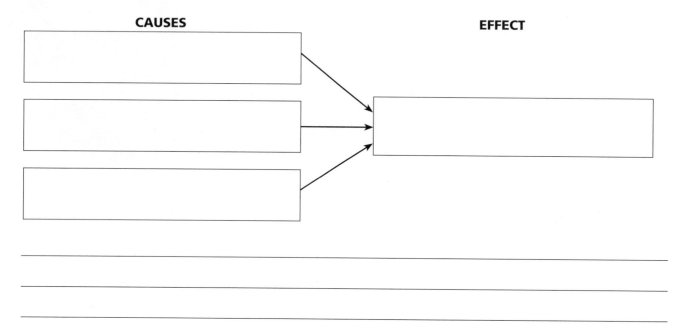

CAUSES   EFFECT

_____

_____

_____

_____

_____

2. What are some effects of violent crime on a community?

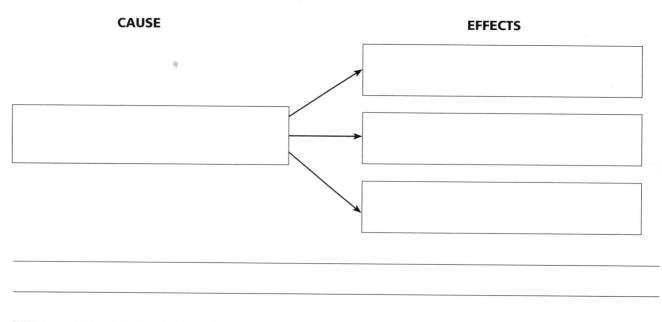

CAUSE   EFFECTS

_____

_____

_____

_____

3. How is the attitude toward domestic violence in the United States similar to the attitude toward it in another country you know? How is it different? Complete the Venn Diagram.

_____
_____
_____
_____
_____

B Create a diagram to organize your ideas in response to the question below. Then write a paragraph.

How can someone become a citizen of the United States?

_____
_____
_____
_____
_____

Community: Rental Agreements

A Look at the definitions below. Read the rental agreement. The vocabulary words are underlined. Write the correct vocabulary word next to each definition.

consent	notice	property	term
deposit	vacate	sublease	utilities

_____ 1. permission or approval

_____ 2. money that you pay when you rent an item or place; you will get the money back if the item or place isn't damaged when you move out

_____ 3. to leave a place so that someone else can occupy it

_____ 4. a building and/or a piece of land

_____ 5. a written announcement or warning

_____ 6. to charge another person to live in a house or apartment that you are renting

_____ 7. the length of time

_____ 8. services like water and electricity

Rental Agreement

1. Parties
The parties in this agreement are hereinafter called "Landlord," _____, and "Tenant," _____.

2. Property
The address of the <u>property</u> is _____
_____
The following furniture and appliances are on said property:_____
_____

3. <u>Term</u>
The agreement is month-to-month, starting on: _____

4. Rent
The monthly rental for said property is $_____, which is due on the_____ of each month.

5. <u>Utilities</u> and Services
Landlord agrees to pay for the following (check all that apply): ☐ Electricity, ☐ Gas, ☐ Water, ☐ Garbage Removal and Recycling, ☐ Cable TV, and ☐ Wi-fi.

6. Security/Cleaning <u>Deposit</u>
Tenant will pay the following amount as a security deposit: $_____.
This deposit will be refunded within 30 days after tenant <u>vacates</u> the premises.

7. Tenant shall not <u>sublease</u> the premises without prior written <u>consent</u> of the landlord.

8. Landlord may enter the premises for the purpose of inspection or maintenance. Except in cases of emergency, Landlord must give Tenant at least 24 hours' <u>notice</u> before entering premises.

9. Upon termination of this agreement, Tenant shall vacate and return premises in the same condition that it was in at the start of the agreement, except for normal wear and tear.

B Complete the sentences with the words from Activity A.

1. The _____ of your rental agreement is six months, starting in January.

2. Does your landlord pay for _____ like water and recycling?

3. I have to pay $1,300 to move into my new apartment. That's $1,000 for rent and $300 for the security _____.

4. You have to give landlords _____ before you move out. You usually have to tell them 30 days before you are ready to leave.

5. I own this _____. I bought the building five years ago.

6. Most landlords don't allow their renters to _____ their apartments. Landlords don't want people other than their renters to live in the apartments.

7. Before you _____ an apartment, you should clean it well. If the apartment is dirty when you leave, your landlord can charge you for cleaning.

8. Did your landlord give his _____ for you to get a pet, or did he say that you can't have one?

C Use the information below to complete the rental agreement in Activity A.

Tenant: Andrew Martin

Landlord: Laura King

Property Address: 3320 Lincoln Avenue
Los Angeles, CA 90230

Move-in Date: August 1, 2012

Rent: $1,095/month; due 1st of the month

Utilities Paid: water; garbage and recycling removal

Deposit: $350

D Practice the conversation below with a partner.

Renter: Do you pay for any utilities?

Landlord: Yes, I pay for water and garbage removal.

Renter: How much is the security deposit?

Landlord: It's $350.

Renter: That's not bad.

Landlord: What do you think? Would you like to rent the apartment?

Renter: Yes, I would.

COMMUNICATION STRATEGY
Agreeing to Terms
Use these phrases when you accept terms of an agreement but don't want to sound too enthusiastic.
That's not bad.
That's fair.
That seems fine.
That sounds OK.

E Now practice the conversation again.
Replace the underlined words with your own ideas. For example, you can ask about rent, specific utilities, term, pet policy, sublease policy, and so on. Use the Conversation Strategy to agree to the terms.

Work: Worker Protection Laws

A Read the questions in the chart below and write your guesses in column 2.

1 Questions	2 My guesses before reading the text	3 Answers from the text
a) Twenty-five-year-old Sandra is a cashier in a large store. Last week her boss asked her to help unpack boxes in the storeroom. Sandra doesn't think she should have to do this because it's not in her job description. Is she right?		
b) Fong works from Wednesday through Sunday. A friend told him that he should get extra pay when he works on the weekend. Is his friend correct?		
c) Selena earns $10.00 an hour, and last week she worked for 45 hours. How much money should her employer pay her for the week?		
d) Twelve-year-old Jesse wants to earn some money so she can take dance lessons. What types of work can she do?		
e) Sixteen-year-old Andy is trying to save money for college. What types of jobs can he do?		

B Read the information below and look for answers to the questions in Activity A. Then write the answers in column 3 of the chart on page 108.

Can an employee be required to do work that is not in the employee's job description?

Yes. The Fair Labor Standards Act (FLSA) does not limit the types of work employees age 18 and older may be asked to do. However, there are limits on the types of work that employees under the age of 18 can do.

Is extra pay required for weekend or night work?

Employers are not required to pay employees extra when they work on weekends or nights. The Fair Labor Standards Act (FLSA) does not require extra pay for weekend or night work. However, the FLSA does require that covered, nonexempt workers be paid not less than time and one-half the employee's regular rate for time worked over 40 hours in a workweek.

When must breaks and meal periods be given?

The Fair Labor Standards Act (FLSA) does not require breaks or meal periods be given to workers. Some states may have requirements for breaks or meal periods. If you work in a state that does not require breaks or meal periods, these benefits are a matter of agreement between the employer and the employee (or the employee's representative).

What is the youngest age at which a person can be employed?

The Fair Labor Standards Act (FLSA) sets 14 as the minimum age for most non-agricultural work. However, at any age, youth may deliver newspapers; perform in radio, television, movie, or theatrical productions; work in businesses owned by their parents (except in mining, manufacturing, or hazardous jobs); and perform babysitting or perform minor chores around a private home. Also, at any age, youth may be employed as homeworkers to gather evergreens and make evergreen wreaths.

Different age requirements apply to the employment of youth in agriculture. Many states have enacted child labor laws, some of which may have a minimum age for employment which is higher than the FLSA. Where both the FLSA and state child labor laws apply, the higher minimum standard must be obeyed.

Source: http://www.dol.gov

Practice Test

DIRECTIONS: Read the article to answer the next five questions. Use the Answer Sheet.

California Speed Laws

In California, the speed limit in residential and business zones is 30 miles per hour unless otherwise posted. School zones are 15 miles per hour unless otherwise posted. This speed limit is observed 30 minutes before to 30 minutes after school is in session.

Maximum safe speed on highways is 65 miles per hour. Certain limited access highways may have a posted limit of 75 mph in specific areas. However, unless posted, you should observe a speed limit of no more than 65 mph.

Your maximum safe driving speed is always determined by the road and weather conditions. The posted speed limit is the maximum speed that is ever allowed, and it may not be appropriate for all conditions. You can get a speeding ticket for driving at the posted limit if conditions are unsafe, for example in snow, rain, or ice.

Fines will be doubled if there are construction workers in a work zone, or if children are present in a school zone.

---

1. When should you drive <u>below</u> the speed limit?

   A. when it is snowing

   B. when the road is in bad condition

   C. when you can't see

   D. all of the above

2. What is the usual speed limit on highways?

   A. 70

   B. 75

   C. 65

   D. 30

3. When do you have to pay twice as much in fines?

   A. when workers or children are present in the zone

   B. when you go twice the speed limit

   C. when the conditions are unsafe

   D. when you are on the highway

4. What is the speed limit in residential zones?

   A. 65 mph

   B. 30 mph

   C. 15 mph

   D. 75 mph

5. Under what condition do you have to drive 15 mph in a school zone?

   A. in bad weather

   B. at night

   C. 30 minutes before school to 30 minutes after school is over

   D. all the time

ANSWER SHEET

	A	B	C	D
1	Ⓐ	Ⓑ	Ⓒ	Ⓓ
2	Ⓐ	Ⓑ	Ⓒ	Ⓓ
3	Ⓐ	Ⓑ	Ⓒ	Ⓓ
4	Ⓐ	Ⓑ	Ⓒ	Ⓓ
5	Ⓐ	Ⓑ	Ⓒ	Ⓓ
6	Ⓐ	Ⓑ	Ⓒ	Ⓓ
7	Ⓐ	Ⓑ	Ⓒ	Ⓓ
8	Ⓐ	Ⓑ	Ⓒ	Ⓓ
9	Ⓐ	Ⓑ	Ⓒ	Ⓓ
10	Ⓐ	Ⓑ	Ⓒ	Ⓓ

DIRECTIONS: Read the website information to answer the next five questions. Use the Answer Sheet on page 110.

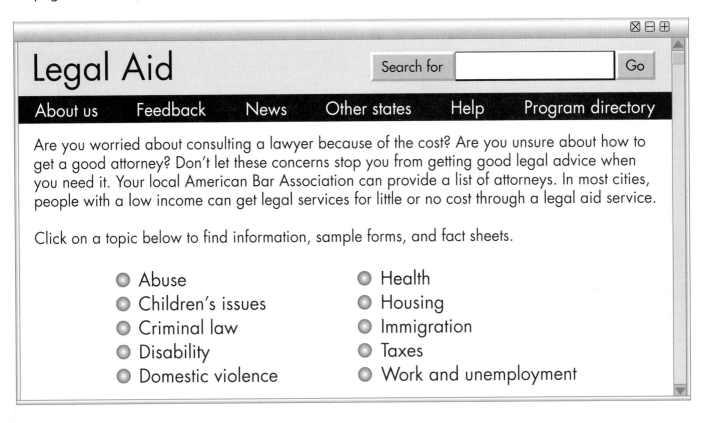

6. Where can some people get legal assistance for free?

   A. American Bar Association

   B. legal aid service

   C. through the telephone directory

   D. through a program directory

7. According to the information, why do people not get legal help?

   A. They don't think they need it.

   B. They are immigrants.

   C. They think it will cost too much.

   D. They are afraid.

8. Who can get legal assistance for little or no cost?

   A. anyone

   B. immigrants

   C. lawyers

   D. people with little money

9. Which of the following is not a topic on the website?

   A. personal injury

   B. work and unemployment

   C. housing

   D. domestic violence

10. What can the Bar Association help you with?

    A. saving money

    B. finding an attorney

    C. talking to legal aid

    D. using a website

HOW DID YOU DO? Count the number of correct answers on your answer sheet. Record this number in the bar graph on the inside back cover.

Solving Problems

A   Look at the photos. Identify a rule the employees are breaking.

John

Scott and Lenny

David

Work Rules

The following are not permitted:

1. fighting
2. being absent without an excuse
3. violating safety rules
4. wearing inappropriate clothing
5. ignoring work duties
6. failing to observe time limits for breaks
7. using office equipment improperly

1. John is _____.

2. Scott and Lenny are _____.

3. David is _____.

B Look at the photos on page 112 again. Read the situations and suggest answers to the questions.

1. Cindy is the owner of a magazine where John works. She comes into the office with a client and finds John making photocopies of money. What should she do?

   _____

   _____

2. Scott and Lenny both want to be chosen to work on a team their boss is putting together. The boss finds them fighting in the hall. What should the boss say to them?

   _____

   _____

3. Meg and David are working on a project together and the deadline is in two days. David is looking at something inappropriate on the computer. What should Meg do?

   _____

   _____

C Read the timeline. Complete the paragraph. Use an appropriate tense of the numbered verb.

	wins Mr. Universe, 1970		becomes naturalized citizen, 1983	marries Maria Shriver, 1986	elected Governor of California, 2003
	moves to the United States, 1968	in movie *Pumping Iron* 1977		becomes Chairman of the President's Council on Physical Fitness and Sports, 1990–1993	

born in Graz, 1947   in movie *Conan the Barbarian* 1982   in movie *Terminator* 1984

Arnold Schwarzenegger _____ (1) born in Graz, Austria, in 1947. He (1) be

_____ (2) to the United States at the age of 21. He first (2) move

_____ (3) famous with the movie *Pumping Iron*. By then, Schwarzenegger (3) become

_____ (4) Mr. Universe, as well as several other body-building titles. (4) win

When he _____ (5) the highly successful movie *Terminator* in 1984, he (5) make

_____ (6) his American citizenship. By the time he _____ (6) recently/get

(7) Maria Shriver, Schwarzenegger _____ (8) in several action (7) marry

movies, but he later _____ (9) in comedies as well. President George (8) already/star

H.W. Bush _____ (10) Schwarzenegger to be Chairman of the (9) act

President's Council on Physical Fitness. On November 17, 2003, Arnold Schwarzenegger (10) appoint

_____ (11) Governor of California. (11) elect

Identifying Job Responsibilities

A Choose the correct form of the words to complete the questions. Then answer the questions.

NOUN	VERB	ADJECTIVE
1. assistant, assistance	assist	XXXXX
2. courtesy	XXXXX	courteous
3. discipline	discipline	disciplinary
4. ignorance	ignore	ignorant
5. possession	possess	possessive
6. preference	prefer	preferable
7. preparation	prepare	preparatory
8. provision, provider	provide	providential
9. recruitment, recruiter	recruit	XXXXX
10. resolution	resolve	resolute

1. What kind of _____ can you give your classmates?

_____

2. Why should salespeople be _____ to customers?

_____

3. What _____ action do you think an employee should face if he or she is drunk at work?

_____

4. What should a supervisor do if employees _____ safety rules?

_____

5. What interpersonal skills do you think a manager should _____?

_____

6. What type of job would you_____?

_____

7. What kind of _____ would you need for your ideal job?

_____

8. Why should an employer _____ benefits?

_____

9. How should employers _____ qualified applicants?

_____

10. If you had a problem with a coworker, how would you _____ it?

_____

B Read the job responsibilities and complete the Venn Diagram below.

Administrative Assistant	Chief Clerk
• Maintains administrative and personnel files • Maintains systems, procedures, and methods for record keeping • Prepares financial reports and budgets • Interacts with vendors, member agencies, and the public to answer questions and to resolve account and billing discrepancies • Writes reports • Handles questions and concerns of employees, officials, and businesses • Assists supervisor as needed • May supervise volunteers and other support personnel	• Prepares special reports and tabulations according to general directions • Edits reports for completeness and accuracy • Maintains personnel records • Keeps records of leave and nontaxable wages • May prepare and distribute paychecks • Compiles information and records to prepare purchase orders • May compare prices and specifications • Maintains cost records on equipment • Assists supervisor as needed

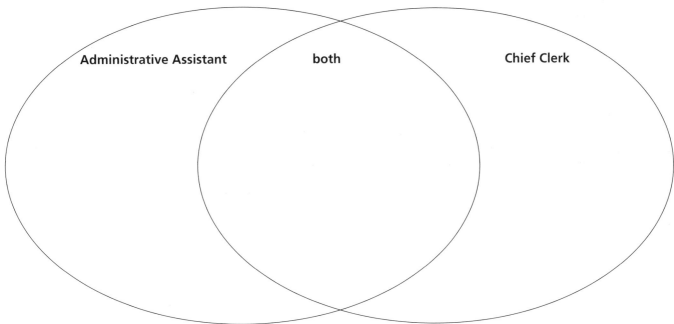

Administrative Assistant   both   Chief Clerk

C Answer the questions.

1. Which job above do you think has more responsibility? Why?

_____

_____

2. Which job above do you think requires more math? Why?

_____

_____

Understanding Job Applications

A Match the questions and the expanded answers. Write the letters on the lines.

1. Why did you leave your last position? _____
2. Did you enjoy working there? _____
3. Where did you work before that? _____
4. Do you have any supervisory experience? _____
5. How long have you lived in the area? _____
6. Can you design websites? _____
7. What did you study in school? _____
8. Have you worked in a real estate office before? _____

a. Business. I graduated from the university in Monterrey.
b. Yes, actually. I worked for my uncle's company one summer and had to design one there.
c. In a clothing store. I was there for a year and a half.
d. Very much. The people were friendly, and the manager gave me a lot of responsibility.
e. No. But I did work in an apartment management office.
f. About two years. I moved here from New York.
g. Yes, I do. I was a shift supervisor at the clothing store.
h. The company relocated, and I didn't want to move.

B Complete the conversations. Expand on your answer.

1. A: Do you like living here?

   B: _____

2. A: Would you like a job working with customers?

   B: _____

3. A: Would you rather work with other people or have more independence?

   B: _____

C Read the interview and answer the questions below.

Interviewer:	I see that you have worked in retail before.
Applicant:	Yeah.
Interviewer:	Could you tell me a little bit about that job?
Applicant:	It was okay. I got to wear what I wanted, and the people were cool.
Interviewer:	What did you do exactly?
Applicant:	Well, I started as, like, a cashier, but after about a year, I got a promotion.
Interviewer:	A promotion?
Applicant:	The manager made me the supervisor of my area. I was responsible for the displays, and I trained the new people.
Interviewer:	Did you like the added responsibility?
Applicant:	You know, I really did. I really like designing stuff, so I enjoyed putting the displays together. And I found out that I like teaching people.
Interviewer:	Well, here we appreciate creativity, but we do have a dress code. Our salespeople would not be allowed to wear an outfit like the one you are wearing now. It's too unconventional.
Applicant:	I've noticed that. But I think if you had your salespeople wear some of the more interesting clothes you carry, you would sell more. Some customers might be afraid to try something off the hanger, but if they see it looks good, they might just try it.

1. How would you describe the applicant's language?
   - ☐ businesslike
   - ☐ casual

2. How was the applicant dressed?
   - ☐ in business attire
   - ☐ casually

3. What is one strength of the applicant?
   - ☐ She's responsible.
   - ☐ She's professional.

4. What is one weakness of the applicant?
   - ☐ She's too informal.
   - ☐ She has a negative attitude.

5. Which description of the applicant is most accurate?
   - ☐ She's friendly.
   - ☐ She's polite.

6. Why would she be good working in a clothing store?
   - ☐ She's well-dressed.
   - ☐ She has good, creative ideas.

7. Would you hire the applicant? Why or why not? _____

_____

_____

_____

_____

Exploring Job Benefits

A Complete the sentences with the words in the box.

401k	dental insurance	flex time	on-site training
on-site child care	paid family leave	personal days	telecommuting

1. Does your job provide _____? Or do you take your children to day care?

2. How many _____ do you get? At my job, we get three weeks for vacations and sick days.

3. My _____ pays 100 percent of the cost of check-ups, but it doesn't pay anything for braces.

4. Does your company provide _____ for computers, or do I have to take a separate computer class?

5. Does your benefits package include _____? My wife and I are expecting a baby in six months.

6. Some days I work from 9:00 to 5:00, and some days I work from 11:00 to 7:00. I like having

   _____.

7. _____ has become very popular. A lot of people work at home and communicate by email and telephone.

8. At my job, I have a _____ to help me save for retirement.

B Read the conversation below. Then practice the conversation with a partner.

A: Do you have any questions about the company?

B: Yes, can you tell me about your benefits package?

A: I'd be happy to. We provide health insurance and dental insurance. We also provide a 401k.

B: How many personal days does the company allow?

A: We allow 15 paid personal days a year.

B: How about family leave and on-site child care?

A: We allow three months of paid family leave per child. I'm afraid that we don't provide child care.

B: Does the company allow flex time and telecommuting?

A: We do allow employees to telecommute, but we don't allow flex time.

C Practice the conversation again. Replace the underlined words with information in the box.

1.	2.	3.
health insurance: yes	health insurance: yes	health insurance: yes
dental insurance: no	dental insurance: yes	dental insurance: yes
401k: yes	401k: no	401k: yes
personal days: 10	personal days: 15	personal days: 20
paid family leave: 4 months	paid family leave: 3 months	paid family leave: 6 months
on-site child care: yes	on-site child care: no	on-site child care: no
flex time: yes	flex time: no	flex time: yes
telecommuting: no	telecommuting: yes	telecommuting: yes

D Read the conversation. Then answer the questions on a separate sheet of paper.

Kathy: Hi, Anna. Can I talk to you about something?

Anna: Sure, Kathy.

Kathy: Something has been bothering me, and I feel that I have to mention it.

Anna: What is it?

Kathy: I've noticed that you take breaks when it's busy. It makes things difficult for the rest of us.

Anna: I'm sorry. I didn't realize that I was doing that. I'll try to take breaks only when it's not busy.

1. What would you do in this situation? Would you talk to Anna? Would you talk to a supervisor instead?

2. Have you ever experienced a problem like this? What did you do?

E Complete each phrasal verb with the correct particle.

Belinda needed money, so she decided to start looking for a job immediately. Yesterday, she

picked _____*up*_____ an application at the new supermarket. She went home right away and filled
　　　　　　　　①

it _____ and dropped it _____ at the store. This morning the store manager called
　　　　②　　　　　　　　　　　　　　③

her _____ and asked her to come _____ for an interview.
　　　④　　　　　　　　　　　　　　　⑤

She showed _____ for the interview several minutes early. At 3:00 the manager interviewed
　　　　　　⑥

her and offered her a night job as a cashier. Belinda thought it _____ for a few minutes and
　　　　　　　　　　　　　　　　　　　　　　　　　　⑦

accepted the offer. She knows she got the job because she followed _____ on her goal and did
　　　　　　　　　　　　　　　　　　　　　　　　　　　　　⑧

not waste time.

Reading: Identifying a Sequence of Events

A Complete the sentences with the correct word or phrase to indicate the sequence of events.

first	finally	today	then	after	before
during	while	meanwhile	when	after that	

_____ I decided to make a special dessert, nut meringue pie.
①
_____ my childhood, my mother always made it for me on my birthday.
②
So I called her and got the recipe. _____ things started to go wrong.
③
_____, I drove to the store and had a flat tire. _____
④   ⑤
I fixed the flat and went to the store, I found out I didn't have my checkbook. _____
⑥
I could pay for the ingredients, I had to go all the way back home. _____, it
⑦
had started snowing and the streets were slippery. _____ I hit the brakes
⑧
suddenly, the eggs flew out of the carton. _____ I had to stop and clean
⑨
up the eggs. Of course, I had to go back to the store for more eggs. _____,
⑩
I made it home with the ingredients, only to find the electricity was out!

B Create a timeline for the story in Activity A.

C Read this story by Aesop and underline the words that help you follow the sequence of events.

The Lion and the Mouse

Once when a lion was asleep, a little mouse began running up and down upon him; this soon wakened the lion, who placed his huge paw upon him and opened his big jaws to swallow him. "Pardon, O King," cried the little mouse: "forgive me this time, and I shall never forget it: who knows but what I may be able to do you a turn some of these days?" The lion was so tickled at the idea of the mouse being able to help him that he lifted up his paw and let him go. Some time after, the lion was caught in a trap, and the hunters, who desired to carry him alive to the King, tied him to a tree while they went in search of a wagon to carry him on. Just then the little mouse happened to pass by, and seeing the sad plight in which the

lion was, went up to him and soon gnawed away the ropes that bound the King of the Beasts. "Was I not right?" said the little mouse.

"Little friends may prove great friends."

D Rewrite the story in your own words.

_____

_____

_____

_____

_____

_____

_____

_____

_____

_____

_____

121

Writing: Writing a Résumé

A Answer the questions about writing a resume.

1. What types of information can you include in your resume?

_____   _____   _____   _____

2. What verb tense should you use for the job you have now? _____

3. What verb tense should you use for jobs that you had before now? _____

4. Which job should you list first, your first job or your most recent job? _____

B Read the information about Tina. Underline the information that should be included in her resume.

Tina March lives in San Diego, California. Her address is 3234 Mission Street, Apt. 7. Her zip code is 92139. She likes to play sports, go to the beach, and spend time with her friends. She is single and doesn't have any children.

Tina just graduated from community college. She just got an Associate's Degree in physical education. She is looking for a job as a physical education teacher for high school students.

Tina has a job right now. She works at Mission Street Community Center. She is the manager of the Sports Center. She has had this job since 2009. Her job responsibilities include managing 14 staff members, teaching volleyball, basketball, and tennis classes to children and adults, running weekly staff meetings to discuss problems, and raising money for the Sports Center. Her favorite part of the job is teaching the classes. Several of the children that she works with have moved to San Diego from Mexico and China and have difficulty with English. Tina speaks Cantonese and Spanish with them.

Before this job, Tina worked at Mike's Gym. She was a personal trainer. She worked with clients several times a week. She created exercise plans for them. Tina has an Associate's Degree in Nutrition, so she used to create eating plans for her clients, too. Three times a week, Tina taught a yoga class. People liked working with Tina because she has excellent interpersonal skills. She really liked the job, but she decided that she wanted to work with children, so she quit. She had that job from 2006 to 2009.

From 2004 to 2006, Tina worked at Solano Sporting Goods. She was a sales associate. When she worked at the store, she could get a 10% discount on anything in the store. In this position, Tina sold exercise equipment and clothing to customers. She also taught people how to use exercise equipment. She really enjoyed working with the customers.

C Use the information from Activity B to write Tina's resume.

———————————
———————————
———————————

EDUCATION

———————————————————————————————
———————————————————————————————

EXPERIENCE

———————————————————————————————
———————————————————————————————

- ——————————————————————————
- ——————————————————————————
- ——————————————————————————

———————————————————————————————
———————————————————————————————

- ——————————————————————————
- ——————————————————————————
- ——————————————————————————

———————————————————————————————
———————————————————————————————

- ——————————————————————————
- ——————————————————————————
- ——————————————————————————

SPECIAL SKILLS

———————————————————————————————
———————————————————————————————
———————————————————————————————
———————————————————————————————

Work: Workforce Trends

A Study the charts and read the sentences below. Check (✓) *True* or *False*.

		True	False
1.	These charts show what might happen in the workforce in the future.	☐	☐
2.	These charts give information about the workforce for the next twenty years.	☐	☐
3.	Chart 1 says that by 2016 there might be a need for about 385,000 more home health aides in the U.S. workforce.	☐	☐
4.	According to Chart 2, there will be about 9,000 fewer positions for farmers and ranchers in the U.S. workforce by 2016.	☐	☐
5.	According to Chart 2, the need for farmers and ranchers will decrease more than the need for sewing machine operators.	☐	☐

Chart 1:

Chart 2:

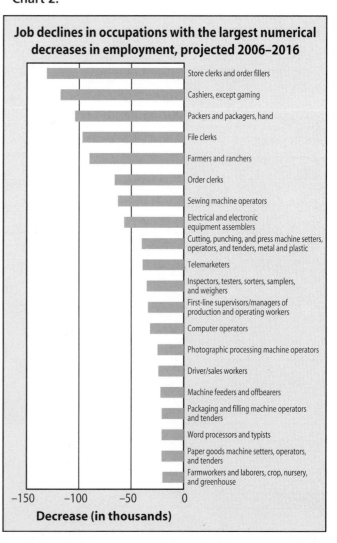

Source: www.bls.gov

B Use the charts on page 124 to answer the questions below. Circle your answers.

1. Which of these occupations will probably employ more people in the future than today?

   A. typists   B. home health aides   C. telemarketers

2. Which of these occupations will probably employ fewer people in the future than today?

   A. medical assistants   B. cashiers   C. computer operators

3. The number of employees in which of these jobs will probably increase the most?

   A. dental hygienists   B. manicurists and pedicurists   C. pharmacy technicians

4. The number of employees in which of these jobs will probably decrease the most?

   A. computer operators   B. cashiers   C. order clerks

C What advice would you give to each of these people?

1. Anita, a high school student, is interested in working with animals. What career planning advice could you give her? Why?

   Your advice:

2. Pépé would like to have a job working with people. He's especially interested in working in health care. What career planning advice could you give him? Why?

   Your advice:

Work: Job Reports

A Read the conversation and practice with a partner. Then complete the weekly report below with information from the conversation.

A: Hello, William. Were you able to finish your work for the week?

B: I finished most of it, but I need to finish a couple of things next week.

A: Did you take inventory?

B: I counted the inventory in the stockroom. But I didn't finish doing inventory on the sales floor.

A: How about deliveries?

B: I delivered two refrigerators this week. But I couldn't deliver the stove. The customer is on vacation until next week.

A: OK. Did you repair Mr. Jackson's refrigerator?

B: Yes, I did that on Tuesday.

A: Great. Were you able to finish training your new assistant?

B: I'm almost finished training him, but I'm going to teach him how to use the cash register on Monday.

A: Good. It sounds like you had a productive week. Have a good weekend.

Weekly Report	Employee: _William Long_
TASK	**PROGRESS**
Inventory	finished stockroom, but didn't finish sales floor
Deliveries	
Repairs	
Training	

B Read the accident report. Then complete the conversation below with information from the report. Practice the conversation with a partner.

ACCIDENT REPORT

You must complete this form within 24 hours of injury to file a claim.

EMPLOYEE SECTION: Complete, sign, and give to supervisor.

Name: Lupe Montes   Job Title: Administrative Assistant

Location Where Injury Occurred: the employee break room

Today's Date: November 2, 2012   Date of Injury: November 1, 2012   Time of Injury: 12:45 P.M.

What were you doing before the accident? I was waiting to wash my lunch dishes and talking to some co-workers. Someone else was washing her dishes.

How and why were you injured? I reached into the sink to pick up the sponge, and I didn't realize there was a knife under it. When I picked up the sponge, I picked up the knife, too, and it cut my hand.

Injuries: Cuts on two fingers of my right hand

Lupe: Ms. Garza? I need to go to the hospital for stitches. I just _____.
①

Supervisor: You cut your _____? How did that
②
happen?

Lupe: I was in _____.
③
I reached _____.
④

Supervisor: And what time did this happen?

Lupe: It happened about 12:45. _____.
⑤

Supervisor: So where were the cuts?

Lupe: On two fingers of _____.
⑥

Supervisor: I'll have someone drive you to the hospital.

Practice Test

DIRECTIONS: Read the job descriptions to answer the next 5 questions. Use the Answer Sheet on page 129.

ADMINISTRATIVE ASSISTANT

Responsibilities:

- Assist department chair
- Update classes in mainframe computer
- Maintain student records
- Submit end-of-term forms, including grades and attendance records
- Assist instructors with forms

Skills:

Can use office software; previous experience in office setting

Salary: $12 an hour

FINANCIAL AID COUNSELOR

Responsibilities:

- Meet with and counsel students on financial aid process
- Review financial aid applications
- Maintain student financial aid records in mainframe computer
- Oversee work-study positions as needed

Skills:

B.A. required in business, education, or counseling; 2 years' experience in higher ed. setting

Salary: $30,000 annually

CASHIER

Responsibilities:

- Handle tuition payments, including cash, check, or credit payments
- Maintain records
- Handle customer questions and concerns
- Count and balance money, prepare deposits

Skills:

1 year's experience as cashier

Salary: $10 an hour

REGISTRAR

Responsibilities:

- Maintain student registration records
- Use computer registration system
- Handle student questions, concerns, complaints
- Provide excellent service

Skills:

B.A. in administration required, M.A. preferred, plus 3 years' experience in educational setting

Salary: $35,000+

1. Which job is the highest paying?

   A. Administrative assistant
   B. Cashier
   C. Financial aid counselor
   D. Registrar

2. Which job has the lowest salary?

   A. Administrative assistant
   B. Cashier
   C. Financial aid counselor
   D. Registrar

3. Which job does not require computer use?

   A. Administrative assistant
   B. Cashier
   C. Financial aid counselor
   D. Registrar

4. Which job requires the most experience?

   A. Administrative assistant
   B. Cashier
   C. Financial aid counselor
   D. Registrar

5. Which job asks for the most education?

   A. Administrative assistant
   B. Cashier
   C. Financial aid counselor
   D. Registrar

DIRECTIONS: Read the article to answer the next 5 questions. Use the Answer Sheet.

How to Get That Job

Your job hunt is a process that can take a long time. Once you have decided on a career and have focused on particular employers, you should prepare for the interview.

- Research the potential employer. You can talk to people in the field, go online, or go to the library to find out as much as possible about the organization. This kind of research will help you ask good questions and will show that you are well-informed. You can also learn if the employer offers good benefits.
- Present yourself in the best possible way. Dress neatly and in a professional manner. Arrive a few minutes before the interview. Be friendly and polite to everyone you meet, including the receptionist.
- Be positive in the interview. Focus on your strengths and how you are working to change any possible weaknesses. Be honest.
- Bring the names and contact information of possible references with you in case you are asked for references.

ANSWER SHEET

1 A B C D
2 A B C D
3 A B C D
4 A B C D
5 A B C D
6 A B C D
7 A B C D
8 A B C D
9 A B C D
10 A B C D

6. What is one way to prepare good questions to ask an interviewer?
   A. arrive early
   B. do research online
   C. focus on your strengths
   D. learn if they offer good benefits

7. Who should you be friendly to?
   A. the interviewer
   B. the supervisor
   C. the receptionist
   D. everyone

8. What should you bring with you?
   A. names of people who know you
   B. names and contact information for references
   C. information on benefits
   D. an application form

9. Which is **not** true?
   A. You should talk mostly about your strengths, not your weaknesses.
   B. You should be honest about areas you are not strong in.
   C. You should dress neatly.
   D. You shouldn't ask questions.

10. What should you do first?
    A. choose a career
    B. research employers
    C. dress well
    D. arrive a little early

HOW DID YOU DO? Count the number of correct answers on your answer sheet. Record this number in the bar graph on the inside back cover.

Budget Planning

A Look at the items Sandy paid for yesterday. Write the amounts in the appropriate places on her monthly expense record below.

| $45.00 | $4.79 | $2.50 | $9.50 | $6.75 |

TRANSPORT.		FOOD		ENTERTAIN.		MISC.		CLOTHING	
5/1 bus pass	$40.00	5/3 groceries	$275.00	5/10 concert	$32.00	5/5 books	$33.80	5/6 skirt	$38.00
5/16 parking	$6.00	5/12 lunch	$11.50	5/12 DVD	$4.25	5/11 shampoo	$3.00	5/6 T-shirt	$15.00
5/24 taxi	$7.30	5/22 groceries	$25.00	5/26 DVD	$4.25	5/16 cards	$5.75	5/20 jacket	$59.00
5/27		5/27		5/27		5/27		5/27	
Total =		Total =		Total =		Total =		Total =	

B Answer the questions about Sandy's purchases and budget.

1. Sandy budgeted $50 for entertainment this month. Is her actual spending over or under budget now? _____

2. She has a monthly spending goal of $200 or less on clothes. What will she have to do to meet this goal? _____

3. If Sandy wanted to reduce her spending, what do you think she could have done without? _____

4. Approximately what percentage of Sandy's total expenses so far this month has been spent on food? _____

C Classify the following expenses into fixed (the same every month) or variable (can change every month) expenses.

mortgage payment	school loan payments	groceries	car payments
gas	utilities	child care	clothing
health insurance	rent	entertainment	bus pass

FIXED	VARIABLE

D Complete the chart with the correct form of the words. Then complete the questions below and answer them.

NOUN	VERB	ADJECTIVE
1.	entertain	entertaining
2.	utilize	XXXXX
3.	transport	transportable
4. miscellany	XXXXX	
5.	clothe	clothed
6.	invest	XXXXX
7. budget		budgeted

1. How much did you spend on _____ last month?

_____

2. Are your _____ higher or lower in the summer?

_____

3. What form of _____ do you usually take to school?

_____

4. What _____ expenses did you have last week?

_____

5. Who spends the most on _____ in your household?

_____

6. What kind of _____ do you have?

_____

7. How much money do you _____ for food every month?

_____

Understanding Financial Terms

A Complete the sentences with a word or phrase from the box.

certificate of deposit	deficit	penalty	fixed	maxed out
withdraw	inflation	full	balance	pay

1. The interest rate on a _____ is higher than on a regular savings account.

2. If you _____ your credit card bill in _____, you don't pay any interest.

3. Although adjustable rate mortgages are cheaper right now, in the long run a _____ rate mortgage might save you more money and it's predictable.

4. There's a _____ for bouncing checks.

5. I couldn't buy the video game. I _____ my credit card.

6. If you _____ money from your IRA account, you will have to pay taxes on it.

7. Because of _____, my rent was raised by $50 this year.

B Unscramble the words to write questions about money. Then write the answers.

1. if / don't / what / you / pay / happens / your credit card bill / on time

Question: _____

Answer: _____

2. of / some advantages / what / a CD / are

Question: _____

Answer: _____

3. invest / why / in an IRA / you / should

Question: _____

Answer: _____

4. governments / have / when / a deficit / do

Question: _____

Answer: _____

C Look at the graph to answer the questions below.

Assets and debts for people with incomes between $625,000 and $1 million (2009)

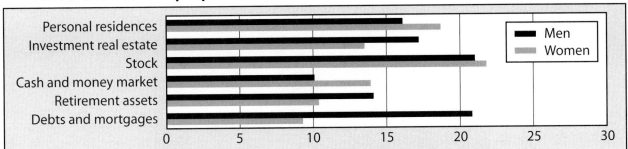

1. For wealthy Americans with incomes between $625,000 and $1 million, who has greater debt (including mortgages), men or women? _____

2. Who has more wealth invested in personal homes? _____

3. Where do wealthy men invest the least? _____

4. Where do wealthy women invest the most? _____

5. Who has more wealth invested in homes that are not for personal use? _____

6. In which asset category are men and women almost equal? _____

D Combine each pair of sentences to make a real conditional sentence with *when* or *if*.

1. You pay $300 a month. You can pay off your debt in two years.

   _____

2. You earn frequent flier miles. You make purchases with this credit card.

   _____

3. You get free online banking. You open this account.

   _____

4. We face inflation. Prices for goods and services rise continuously.

   _____

5. I work overtime every week. I have enough money to eat out on the weekend.

   _____

6. You don't have to pay taxes until you withdraw it. You put money in an IRA account.

   _____

7. You don't pay your credit card bill on time. You pay an interest penalty.

   _____

8. The government has a budget deficit. It spends more than it earns.

   _____

Comparing Banking Services

A Number each conversation in order starting with #1.

Conversation A: BankPlus
___ Well, do you just have one type of checking account?
___ What are the differences?
_1_ Hi. How can I help you?
___ Whoa. What about the free checking account?
___ Hi. I wanted to ask a few questions about opening a checking account.
___ Well, you don't earn interest, but there is no minimum balance and no monthly service fee.
___ I think I'll try that one.
___ No, BankPlus actually offers two types of accounts, free checking and deluxe checking.
___ With deluxe checking you get free checks, and can earn interest, but you must have a minimum balance of $2,500 in your account.
___ Sure. What would you like to know?

Conversation B: Grand Bank
___ The Premium account requires a minimum balance of $1,500. With the Gold Star account, you need to maintain a minimum balance of $5,000, but you earn interest.
___ Sure. I'd be happy to answer your questions. What would you like to know?
___ Does Grand Bank offer free checks with checking accounts?
___ Is there a minimum balance on basic checking?
___ Yes, we do, with our Premium and Gold Star accounts. With basic checking, the first 500 checks are free, but there is a charge for additional checks.
___ No. And there is no monthly service fee, either. The other two charge fees when you drop below the minimums.
_1_ Excuse me. I'd like some information about checking accounts.
___ I think I'd like to open a Premium account.
___ What are some other differences?

B Read the sentences and circle *True* or *False*.

1. The Gold Star account requires a higher minimum balance than BankPlus's
   deluxe checking account.   TRUE   FALSE
2. BankPlus does not offer interest on its checking accounts.   TRUE   FALSE
3. BankPlus offers more types of checking accounts than Grand Bank.   TRUE   FALSE
4. Both banks offer free checks with all accounts.   TRUE   FALSE
5. Grand Bank has a greater range of options than BankPlus.   TRUE   FALSE

C Complete the Venn Diagram to compare the two banks in Activity A.

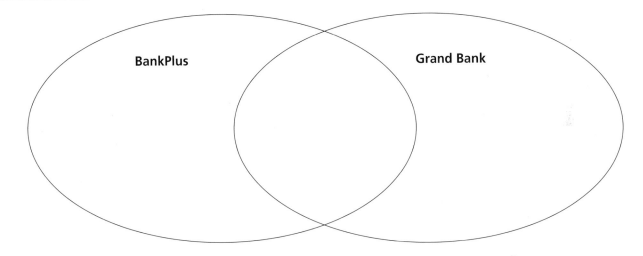

D Write real conditional sentences for a future possibility. Use the words in parentheses.

1. (don't work full time this week)

   _____

2. (spend too much money on entertainment this month)

   _____

   _____

3. (work overtime this month)

   _____

4. (don't pay my bills on time)

   _____

5. (doesn't find a job soon)

   _____

6. (has some extra money at the end of the month)

   _____

   _____

Interpreting Pay Stubs

A Match the words and the definitions.

1. ____ gross pay
2. ____ pay period
3. ____ federal income tax
4. ____ net pay
5. ____ Medicare
6. ____ year-to-date
7. ____ deductions
8. ____ rate

a. the money taken out of your pay
b. the dates for which you are being paid
c. from the beginning of this year until now
d. government health insurance for people 65 and older
e. the total amount of money you earned
f. the tax you pay to the US government
g. the amount you get paid per hour
h. the total amount of money you earned minus deductions

B Look at the pay stub and answer the questions.

MIKE'S GYM

Employee:	Tina March	Check Number: **45336**
Social Security Number:	123-45-6789	
Pay Period Date:	5/1/10 to 5/15/10	
Check Date:	5/16/10	

PAY STUB

EARNINGS	Rate	Hours	This Period	Year-to-Date
	35.00	60	$2,100.00	$18,900.00
GROSS PAY			2,100.00	18,900.00
DEDUCTIONS				
	Federal Income Tax		$312.00	$1,560.00
	Social Security		225.00	1,125.00
	Medicare		51.80	259.00
	CA Income Tax		58.47	292.35
	CA State Disability Ins.		30.50	152.50
Total Deductions			$677.77	$3,388.85
NET PAY			$1,422.23	$7,111.15

C Complete each sentence with information from Tina's pay stub.

1. Tina's gross pay between May 1 and May 15 was _____.

2. This pay stub is for _____ weeks of work.

3. So far this year, Tina has earned _____ in gross pay.

4. She has taken home _____ so far this year.

5. Tina paid _____ in Federal Income tax this pay period.

6. Tina has paid _____ in California Income tax so far this year.

7. Tina paid _____ in Social Security deductions this pay period.

8. Tina earns _____ per hour.

9. Tina works about _____ hours per week.

10. Tina's total deductions so far this year amount to _____.

D Tina was sick between 5/16 and 5/30, so she worked only 50 hours during that pay period. Fill in the blanks on Tina's pay stub. You can look at the pay stub on page 136 to help you.

PAY STUB

MIKE'S GYM

Employee:	Tina March	Check Number: **45378**
Social Security Number:	123-45-6789	
Pay Period Date:	5/6/10 to 5/31/10	
Check Date:	6/2/10	

EARNINGS	Rate	Hours	This Period	Year-to-Date
	35.00	50	$ _____	$ _____
GROSS PAY			_____	_____
DEDUCTIONS				
	Federal Income Tax		$273.50	$ _____
	Social Security		201.75	1,326.75
	Medicare		41.60	_____
	CA Income Tax		50.23	_____
	CA State Disability Ins.		25.90	178.40
Total Deductions			$ _____	$ _____
	NET PAY		$ _____	$ _____

Reading: Identifying Elements of a Story

A Read the story and answer the questions on page 139.

A Baker's Wish

May Brown lived with her father above their bakery in the middle of a very busy town. Every morning, May would force herself out of bed several hours before the sun came up, quickly get dressed, and go downstairs to help her father bake bread.

As soon as the sun came up, the townspeople would crowd the little bakery, pushing and shoving to be served first. Tired and in a bad mood, May would scowl at them and think, "If I were a customer here, I would wait patiently instead of pushing and shoving."

Because the Browns were the only bakers in town, they had to bake enough bread for the whole town. "If there were another baker in town, we wouldn't have to make so much bread," May said to her father one morning. "And if we didn't have to make so much bread, we would be able to sleep a little longer."

"I wouldn't mind having a little less business, but be careful what you wish for, May," her father said, looking exhausted.

A few weeks later, when May went to the front of the shop to open the doors in the morning, she found that no one was waiting outside. Curious, she stepped outside to look around. Townspeople were coming out of a building down the street with loaves of bread under their arms. There was a new bakery in town!

"Why have they all gone to the new bakery?" May asked her father. "I thought we might lose a few customers if there were a new bakery in town, but I didn't think we would lose all of them." Her father just shrugged his shoulders and continued baking.

As the days passed, May's father stopped baking, and he looked miserable and worried all the time. May became more and more concerned about him. Finally, she walked over to the new bakery one morning to find out why everyone seemed to like it better than the old bakery. When she got there, all of the customers were having pleasant conversations and patiently waiting their turn. May waited outside until all of the customers had left. Then she went in and pretended she was a customer. "May I have a loaf of bread?" she asked.

The young baker looked exhausted. "Of course," he said, smiling, and handed her a nicely wrapped loaf of warm bread.

"Thank you." May paid him and began to leave. But then she turned back toward him and said, "I know you must be exhausted, but you're very polite."

"Well, exhaustion is no excuse to be rude to my customers," the baker said. "One of my customers told me that they prefer my bakery because the young woman at the other bakery is rude. But I wish she weren't. If she were nicer, I wouldn't have so many customers. And if I didn't have so many customers, I wouldn't have to bake so much bread," he said, flopping onto a chair.

Embarrassed, May flopped onto the chair next to the baker. "I'm that rude young woman," she confessed. "I didn't mean to be rude. I was just so tired all the time."

"I have an idea," the young baker said. "Tomorrow, I'll bake only enough bread for half of the town. You bake enough for the other half. Then half the townspeople will be forced to go to your bakery. And if you're polite to them, they'll keep coming back."

"That's a great idea," May said. Smiling, she shook the young baker's hand. Then she went home and told her father the whole story. The next day, everything went just as May and the young baker had planned. That evening, May's father invited the young baker to dinner to celebrate their new situation. And the next morning, they all got a couple extra hours of sleep.

B Answer the questions about the story on page 138.

1. Who is the main character in the story? _____

2. Write three adjectives to describe the main character.

_____   _____   _____

3. What is the setting for the story?

_____

4. What is the conflict in the story?

_____

_____

_____

5. Circle the paragraph where the climax of the story happens. Describe the climax.

_____

_____

_____

6. How is the conflict resolved?

_____

_____

C The lesson of the story "A Baker's Wish" is that you must be careful what you wish for. Do you agree? Write a short paragraph in which you say why you agree or disagree with this lesson. Support your opinion with examples.

_____

_____

_____

_____

_____

_____

_____

_____

_____

Writing: Using Transition Words and Phrases

A Write the transition words and phrases in the appropriate places in the chart.

also	and	as a result	conversely
besides	but	consequently	first
despite	due to	even though	further
for example	for instance	for this reason	instead of
furthermore	however	in addition	nevertheless
in spite of	like	moreover	such as
on the other hand	second	so	thus
therefore	third	yet	
too	whereas	because	

To add information	To show order	To show cause and effect

To give an example	To show a contrast	

B Complete the paragraph with appropriate transition words.

I'd like to give some advice to the immigrants in the community: be careful. There are a lot of crooks out there who will take advantage of you. _____ you don't know the culture (1) or the language very well, you are very easy victims. People might try to cheat you on big purchases _____ (2) cars. _____ , the (3) salesperson might tell you it's a really low price, _____ then you find out later that you are going to be paying for it for a very (4) long time. _____ other people may try to get you to pay for special classes. (5) _____ some businesses and organizations say they really want to help immigrants, (6) they may try to cheat you, _____ , I encourage you to take English classes. (7) _____ relying on advertisements, find out about businesses from the Better Business (8) Bureau.

C Write a paragraph about a problem you have had with a purchase. Use transition words and phrases.

_____

_____

_____

_____

_____

_____

_____

_____

Family: Utilities and Bills

A Read the conversation with a partner.

A: Good morning. <u>Pacific Cable Company</u>. How can I help you?

B: Hi, I'd like to have cable installed* in my home.

A: OK. When would you like that service to start?

B: I'd like it to start <u>as soon as possible</u>.

A: We can send someone out to your apartment <u>next Monday between 8:00 A.M. and noon</u>. Will that work for you?

B: No, I won't be home on <u>Monday</u>. Can you send someone on <u>Tuesday morning</u> instead?

A: Yes, we can send someone on <u>Tuesday between 10:00 A.M. and 2:00 P.M.</u>

B: That's great. Thank you.

---

*Useful Expressions

to get household utilities

have cable installed

have the gas turned on

have the power turned on

get telephone service

get Internet access

B Now practice the conversation again. Replace the underlined words with your own ideas.

C Look at the telephone bill. Then answer the questions below.

United Telephone Company

Contact Information:
1-800-555-8989

Page: 1 of 5
Billing Cycle: 10/06/12–11/05/12
Account Number: 818-555-0909

Previous Balance	44.95
Payment Received	–44.95
Monthly Service Charges	12.99
Usage Charges	2.22
Credits/Adjustments/Other Charges	8.43
Government Fees & Taxes	6.36
Long-Distance Total	8.27

TOTAL CURRENT CHARGES   38.27
Due: Nov. 25, 2012
Late fees assessed after Dec. 05

Linda Ono
1145 Green Street
Los Angeles, CA 90068

TOTAL AMOUNT DUE   38.27

---

1. What is the telephone number of the telephone company? _____

2. What dates are included in this bill? _____

3. How much was paid last month? _____

4. How much is due this month? _____

5. How much is the long-distance total? _____

6. When is the payment due? _____

D There have been mistakes on Linda's phone bill lately, so she has been keeping a list of telephone calls she makes. Compare the handwritten list of telephone calls and the calls on the telephone bill. Circle the mistakes on the telephone bill.

Oct. 10	11:08PM–11:11PM	Carla: 661-555-9042
Oct. 12	9:47AM–9:52AM	Carla: 661-555-9042
Oct. 12	3:18PM–3:32PM	Michael: 213-555-6332
Oct. 16	4:55PM–5:03PM	Lee's Gifts: 415-555-3356
Nov. 2	8:02AM–8:24PM	Jane: 206-555-4763

No.	Date	Time	Location	Number	Min.	Amount
1	10/10	11:08PM	Bakersfield, CA	661-555-9042	3	.27
2	10/12	9:47AM	Bakersfield, CA	661-555-9042	5	.55
3	10/12	3:18PM	Los Angeles, CA	213-555-6332	14	1.54
4	10/14	3:22AM	New York, NY	212-555-4289	65	7.15
5	10/16	4:55PM	San Francisco, CA	415-555-3356	8	.88
6	10/22	9:09PM	Miami, FL	305-555-1173	12	1.08
7	10/28	7:25PM	Los Angeles, CA	213-555-6332	32	2.88
8	10/29	6:45PM	Bakersfield, CA	661-555-9042	18	1.62
9	11/02	8:02AM	Seattle, WA	206-555-4763	22	2.32

E Complete the conversation with information from Activities D and E. Then practice the conversation with a partner.

A: United Telephone. This is Rita speaking. May I have your name and account number please?

B: Hi. My name is _____ (1), and my account number is _____ (2).

A: Thank you, Ms. Ono. How can I help you today?

B: I'm calling about some errors on my bill.*

A: Oh, I'm sorry about that. Let me pull up your most recent bill. OK, here it is. Can you tell me what the errors are?

B: Yes. I didn't call _____ (3). I don't know anyone in New York.

A: OK. And the next one?

B: I didn't call _____ (4). I wasn't home on October 22. I also wasn't home on October 28, so I didn't call _____ (5) that day.

A: All right. Are there any other problems?

B: Yes. The last error is the call on _____ (6). I didn't call Bakersfield that day.

A: Can I put you on hold for a moment while I look into this?

B: OK. Thank you.

*Useful Expressions

to discuss problems with your bill

I'm calling about some errors on my bill.
I'm calling about a problem with my bill.
I'm calling because I found some mistakes on my bill.

Community: Government Debt

A What do you think? Read the statements below and check (✓) *True* or *False* in column 2.

Statements	My answers before reading the article		My answers after reading the article	
	True	False	True	False
1. The U.S. government is in debt now.	☐	☐	☐	☐
2. The U.S. government owes money to other countries.	☐	☐	☐	☐
3. The U.S. government has to pay interest on the national debt.	☐	☐	☐	☐
4. The amount of interest the government pays on the national debt is almost as much as the government pays for defense.	☐	☐	☐	☐
5. The U.S. national debt is the same as the U.S. budget deficit.	☐	☐	☐	☐

B Read the information below to check your answers from Activity A. Then check (✓) the correct answers in Column 3 above.

The U.S. National Debt

The **National Debt** is the total amount of money owed by the government. On August 31, 2009, the National Debt of the United States was $11,738,082,047,654.29. That was the total amount of money that the government owed. It's a lot of money! So if each person in the United States had to pay an equal share of the debt, it would cost each of us $38,225.70. Who exactly do we owe the money to? According to the pie chart in Figure 1, the largest amount of money is owed to the Federal Reserve Bank and to other government accounts. In other words, this is money that the United States borrowed from itself. However, it is money that either we or future generations of Americans have to pay back.

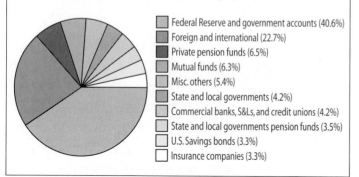

- Federal Reserve and government accounts (40.6%)
- Foreign and international (22.7%)
- Private pension funds (6.5%)
- Mutual funds (6.3%)
- Misc. others (5.4%)
- State and local governments (4.2%)
- Commercial banks, S&Ls, and credit unions (4.2%)
- State and local governments pension funds (3.5%)
- U.S. Savings bonds (3.3%)
- Insurance companies (3.3%)

The U.S. Budget Deficit

The **Federal Budget Deficit** is the difference between the amount of money the government collects and the amount of money it spends in a year. Whenever the government spends more than it collects in a year, it has a budget deficit. Historically, there have been many more budget deficits than budget surpluses (the opposite of a deficit). If you add up all the deficits and subtract the few surpluses for the past 200 years, you get the current National Debt. This is why the U.S. National Debt is so high. In 2008, the federal deficit was $407 billion. Where does the government spend the money? The pie chart in Figure 2 shows where the money goes.

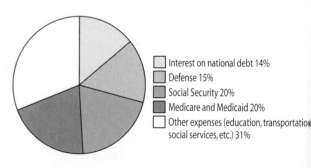

- Interest on national debt 14%
- Defense 15%
- Social Security 20%
- Medicare and Medicaid 20%
- Other expenses (education, transportation, social services, etc.) 31%

"Who We Owe Money To," U.S. National Debt Clock at www.brillig.com. Image courtesy of Ed Hall.

C Answer these questions.

1. If the government collects $1.9 trillion dollars and spends $2 trillion in one year, does it have a surplus or a deficit? _____

2. Let's say that the government spends $2 trillion in one year. If 10% of its expenses are used to pay interest on the national debt, how much money is that? _____

3. Let's say that your expenses for one year came to $30,000. If 15% of your expenses went to paying interest on your debt, how much money would that be? _____

4. What does the chart below tell you about the U.S. national debt? Write 3 things.

   1) _____

   2) _____

   3) _____

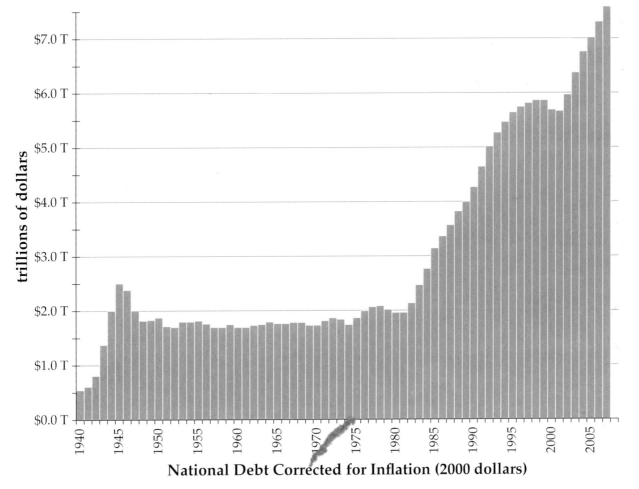

National Debt Corrected for Inflation (2000 dollars)

Source: U.S. National Debt Clock
http://www.brillig.com/debt_clock/

Practice Test

DIRECTIONS: Read the article to answer the next 5 questions. Use the Answer Sheet on page 147.

Payment Methods

There are several different ways to pay for products and services, and they each have advantages and disadvantages. Many people are uncomfortable paying for large items with cash because it can be dangerous to carry around a lot of money. However, cash payments are accepted for most purchases and certainly don't involve paying interest.

Many Americans pay for purchases both large and small with credit. When you use credit, you are basically borrowing money at an interest rate to pay for something. People often use credit cards, especially when they are buying something relatively small, such as clothes or groceries. We also say people are using credit when they take out a loan to buy something big, such as a car. Although credit is convenient, it will usually cost more in the long run.

People also write checks to pay for goods and services. This method does not involve paying interest or carrying around large sums of money. Sometimes people pay a small fee to write a check. Usually you need to have a photo ID if you want to write a check.

Another form of payment is the debit card. It is convenient like a credit card, but unlike credit cards, debit cards draw on existing money in an account, rather than on borrowed money.

Still others use money orders to pay for goods and services, especially if they don't have a checking account. Money orders are often used to pay bills because they can be mailed. You usually pay a fee for a money order. You can buy them at post offices, banks, and some stores.

1. How many payment methods are mentioned?
   A. five
   B. two
   C. three
   D. four

2. Which form of payment is basically borrowing money?
   A. cash
   B. money orders
   C. credit
   D. debit

3. What is one problem with using a credit card?
   A. It's not convenient.
   B. It's not accepted everywhere.
   C. It usually means you pay interest.
   D. You can only use it at post offices and banks.

4. Which form of payment can you buy at some stores?
   A. credit card
   B. debit card
   C. check
   D. money order

5. Which form of payment is most like a credit card in terms of convenience?
   A. credit card
   B. debit card
   C. check
   D. money order

DIRECTIONS: Read the graph to answer the next 5 questions. Use the Answer Sheet.

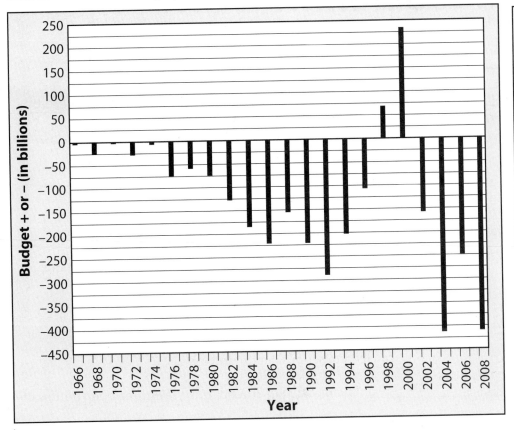

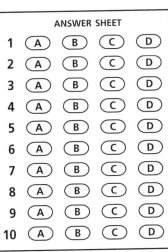

ANSWER SHEET

1 Ⓐ Ⓑ Ⓒ Ⓓ
2 Ⓐ Ⓑ Ⓒ Ⓓ
3 Ⓐ Ⓑ Ⓒ Ⓓ
4 Ⓐ Ⓑ Ⓒ Ⓓ
5 Ⓐ Ⓑ Ⓒ Ⓓ
6 Ⓐ Ⓑ Ⓒ Ⓓ
7 Ⓐ Ⓑ Ⓒ Ⓓ
8 Ⓐ Ⓑ Ⓒ Ⓓ
9 Ⓐ Ⓑ Ⓒ Ⓓ
10 Ⓐ Ⓑ Ⓒ Ⓓ

6. In what year was the U.S. budget deficit the greatest?
   A. 1966
   B. 1972
   C. 1982
   D. 2004

7. In what year was the budget deficit closest to zero?
   A. 1968
   B. 1970
   C. 1980
   D. 1990

8. Between what years was there the greatest change?
   A. between 1994 and 1996
   B. between 1996 and 1998
   C. between 1998 and 2000
   D. between 2000 and 2002

9. In what year did the U.S. economy have the most money?
   A. 2002
   B. 2000
   C. 1998
   D. 1996

10. In which years did the U.S. not have a deficit?
    A. 1968 and 1970
    B. 1978 and 1980
    C. 1988 and 1990
    D. 1998 and 2000

HOW DID YOU DO? Count the number of correct answers on your answer sheet. Record this number in the bar graph on the inside back cover.

Reporting a Problem with Workplace Equipment

A Complete the conversation between two safety inspectors with the words and phrases in the box.

toxic	up to code	hazardous	inadequate ventilation
paper jam	update	goggles	cleanser

A: How's your inspection going?

B: Not very well. There are a lot of serious problems at this work site. It looks like a _____
(1)
place to work. I'm not surprised that so many employees have reported injuries and workplace hazards.

A: I know. I noticed that the ventilation system is really old. It's not _____.
(2)

B: They need to _____ it and get a newer one. The workers need to have clean air
(3)
to breathe. _____ can lead to serious health problems.
(4)

A: There are a lot of _____ chemicals lying around, too. I saw three open bottles of
(5)
_____ in the lunchroom. Those containers are supposed to stay closed unless
(6)
someone is using them to clean the machines.

B: That's terrible. Someone told me that there isn't enough safety equipment for all of the workers. Last week,
someone injured his eye because he wasn't wearing _____.
(7)

A: Well, I think I've finished my part of the report. Let's make a photocopy of it.

B: We can't. The copy machine has a _____.
(8)

A: Well, that's not surprising.

B What kinds of problems should you look out for at your workplace or your school?

_____

_____

_____

_____

_____

_____

C Read about the problem. Then complete a Workplace Hazard Report Form for the problem.

Mark was at work this morning when he slipped and fell on some liquid on the floor. He followed the liquid and saw that it was coming from a large can in the corner. Mark knew that the can contained a mix of used oil and toxic cleansers. It smelled awful. Mark thought that people could get sick if they breathed it.

Workplace Hazard Report Form			
Details of the problem:			
Name the piece of equipment. _____			
Describe the specific problem. _____			
_____			
Check an answer for each question.	Not Likely	Likely	Very Likely
1. Is it likely to delay work?	☐	☐	☐
2. Is it likely to cause injury?	☐	☐	☐
3. Is it likely to make someone ill?	☐	☐	☐
4. Is it likely to kill someone?	☐	☐	☐

D Complete each sentence. Use the correct forms of *wish* and the verb in parentheses.

1. I _____ we _____ (have) some new equipment.
2. I _____ the office _____ (be) cooler.
3. Ray _____ he _____ (not / have to) work on the weekend.
4. Martin _____ he _____ (can buy) a new computer.
5. My boss _____ I _____ (be) on time.
6. The supervisor _____ the workers _____ (not / take) long breaks.
7. I _____ my boss _____ (give) a raise.
8. We _____ we _____ (can get) some more training.

E Each sentence describes something that the speaker wants to change. Write a sentence with *wish* to describe what the speaker wants.

1. I don't have a full-time job.   _____
2. I'm not computer literate.   _____
3. My writing is not very good.   _____
4. I don't have much responsibility at work. _____
   _____
5. I have to work the night shift.   _____
   _____

Discussing a Work Schedule

A Look at the schedule. Check *True* or *False* for each statement.

Day	Morning Shift	Afternoon Shift	Evening Shift
Monday Sept 7	Closed for Labor Day		
Tuesday Sept 8	Mark Cory	Lucy David	Jay Nina
Wednesday Sept 9	Mark Sam	Lucy David	Sam Nina
Thursday Sept 10	Eric Cory	Jay Lucy	David Nina
Friday Sept 11	Kelly Lucy	Jay Sam	Cory David
Saturday Sept 12	Mark Eric	Jay Nina	Kelly Sam
Sunday Sept 13	Cory David	Jay Nina	Kelly Sam

	True	False
1. Mark has the day off on Thursday.	☐	☐
2. Cory works three morning shifts this week.	☐	☐
3. Kelly and Sam always work together.	☐	☐
4. Jay usually works the afternoon shift.	☐	☐
5. Nina has the day off on Wednesday.	☐	☐
6. Kelly had to work the evening shift this weekend.	☐	☐
7. Lucy doesn't have to work on Tuesday.	☐	☐
8. Eric has the afternoon shift on Saturday.	☐	☐

B Complete the conversations with the words in the box..

| the morning shift | early | closed for the holiday | the day off | switch shifts | work for |

Mark: Sam, can you _____(1)_____ with me on Tuesday? I'm going out of town for Labor Day and I'm coming back on Tuesday morning, so I can't work the _____(2)_____.

Sam: Sure, I can do that. Can you _____(3)_____ me on Saturday? I have to go to a wedding on Saturday night.

Mark: No problem.

Lucy: I have to leave _____(4)_____ on Monday. Can you handle the last half hour by yourself?

David: We're _____(5)_____ on Monday. You don't have to come in at all.

Lucy: Oh yeah, I forgot about Labor Day. That's great. It'll be nice to have _____(6)_____.

David: Actually, can you switch shifts with me on Thursday and Friday? I'm taking a computer class and it meets on Thursday and Friday evenings.

Lucy: OK.

C Read the conversations in Activity B again. Make changes to the schedule on page 150.

D Complete the sentences with *will* or *be going to* and the verb in parentheses. Use contractions.

1. A: My wife just called. Our son is sick and I need to go home.

   B: Don't worry. I _____ (cover) for you. I have to be here anyway.

2. A: _____ you _____ (come) to the company picnic this weekend?

   B: No, my friends and I _____ (go camping) this weekend.

3. A: I have to get this report in the mail by 5 pm.

   B: I _____ (take) it to the post office for you. It's on my way home.

4. A: How long _____ your boss _____ (be) away?

   B: About a week. She _____ (visit) the new office in Toronto.

   A: Well, if you need any help while she's gone, I _____ (be) here.

   B: Great. Thanks.

5. A: _____ you _____ (explain) some parts of the contract to me? I don't understand some of it.

   B: Sure. Which parts do you have trouble understanding?

6. A: _____ you _____ (ask) Bob to call me? I haven't been able to reach him all day.

   B: Sure, no problem. I _____ (tell) him when I see him tonight.

Discussing Your Career Path

A Complete the conversation. Use the words and phrases in the box.

team skills	resolve	writing skills
management	what's on your mind	accounting

George: Hi, Sam. Do you have a minute?

Sam: Sure, George. _____ ?

①

George: I'd like to talk about a promotion to assistant manager.

Sam: I see. Can you tell me why you feel you deserve a promotion?

George: OK. First, I have excellent _____. People like working with

me. Second, I'm a good team leader. I helped _____ a

②

③

problem between two coworkers last week. Also, I've been taking a course in

_____ this semester. My teacher says I'm a natural leader.

④

And I'll be taking an _____ course next semester, so I'll be

⑤

able to help you with bills and payroll.

Sam: How are your _____ ? Assistant managers have to answer

⑥

customer emails. And they run errands sometimes. Do you have a driver's license?

George: I'm not a great writer, but I can work on that. I don't know how to drive.

Sam: Well, let me think about all this. I'll get back to you at the end of the week.

George: All right. Thanks for your time, Sam.

B Complete the chart below with information from Activity A.

George's Strengths	George's Areas for Improvement	Next Steps

C Complete the sentences below. Use the information from Activities A and B.

1. I (think / don't think) George will get a promotion because _____

   _____

   _____

2. If George wants a promotion, he should _____

   _____

   _____

3. I (think / don't think) George prepared well for his discussion with Sam because

   _____

   _____

D Use the cues to write sentences with the future continuous.

1. (work on the spreadsheet / after lunch)

   Nancy _____

   _____

2. (install new copy machine / Wednesday afternoon)

   A technician _____

   _____

3. (substitute / for our teacher / for the rest of the year)

   Mr. Cooper _____

   _____

4. (do a presentation / this afternoon)

   We _____

   _____

5. (look for a new receptionist / next month)

   My partner and I _____

   _____

Analyzing Performance Evaluations

A Look at the pictures. Write the correct word or phrase from the box under each picture.

creative   punctual   productive
organized   good interpersonal skills   not cooperative

Sue

Terry

Christina

Mark

Lena

Ken

1. Sue	4. Mark
2. Terry	5. Lena
3. Christina	6. Ken

B Write sentences about each person in Activity A.

1. _____
2. _____
3. _____
4. _____
5. _____
6. _____

C Complete the "Rating" column of Mike's employee performance evaluation. Then answer the questions.

Employee Performance Evaluation

EMPLOYEE		TITLE	
Mike Gomez		Server	

1 = Excellent   2 = Very Good   3 = Satisfactory   4 = Decreased Performance   5 = Unsatisfactory

Job Responsibilities	Rating	Comments
PUNCTUALITY The employee is on time and follows the rules for breaks.	_____	Mike usually arrives about twenty minutes early for his shift.
BEHAVIOR The employee is polite on the job.	_____	Mike is usually polite, but he is occasionally rude to customers who need a lot of extra attention.
INDEPENDENCE The employee accomplishes work with little or no supervision.	_____	Mike studies the menu every day before his shift. If he doesn't understand something on the menu, he asks the chef for clarification.
RELIABILITY The employee can be relied on to efficiently complete a job.	_____	Mike always does his share of the work. When another server is late or can't come in, he can be relied on to help out.

1. What are Mike's greatest strengths on the job?

_____

2. What are Mike's greatest weaknesses on the job?

_____

3. What could Mike do to improve his job performance?

_____

D Complete each sentence with so or such + that.

1. Alan is _____ dependable _____ some of his coworkers expect him to do their work as well.
2. Rita and Jack are _____ creative _____ they write all of the store's ads.
3. It's _____ a good restaurant _____ I go there three times a week.
4. I'm _____ tired _____ I could fall asleep standing up.
5. Marta is _____ a friendly person _____ she gets along with everyone.
6. I was _____ productive today _____ I have no work to do tomorrow!

155

Reading: Highlighting Important Information

A Answer the questions.

1. What kinds of information should you highlight when you are reading?

   _____

2. What two questions can you ask yourself to decide what to highlight?

   _____

   _____

3. How can highlighting be useful at school and in your life in general?

   _____

   _____

B Read the passage on page 157. Highlight or underline the important ideas. Then use the highlighted information to answer the questions below.

1. What can you do to be prepared for a performance review?

   _____

   _____

   _____

2. What are the purposes of a performance review?

   _____

   _____

   _____

3. What should you do if you receive a positive performance review?

   _____

   _____

   _____

4. What should you do if you receive a negative performance review?

   _____

   _____

   _____

The Ins and Outs of Performance Evaluations

Many employers use performance evaluations, or reviews, to assess their employees' performance. Typically, these reviews take place annually, and employees are informed ahead of time that they are going to be evaluated. Although performance reviews can cause anxiety, there are some things that you can do to feel a little less nervous.

Being prepared for your review can help you focus on your achievements rather than on your nerves. It also helps you feel that you have some control over your evaluation. Make a list of your achievements since your last performance review. Next to each achievement, list one or two ways in which your employer has benefited from it. For example, if you solved a complicated problem for a customer, there's a good chance that the customer will keep doing business with your company.

You might wish you didn't have to have a performance review, but this kind of evaluation is a great learning opportunity. Understanding the reasons for the review and the review process can help you get more out of the review. Remember, you aren't being punished. A performance review actually has several purposes. First, it is an opportunity for you and your supervisor to communicate and clarify expectations. Second, a review enables an employer to encourage good performance. Third, a review gives an employee a chance to improve poor performance. Without reviews, employees might not know what they are doing well or what they are doing poorly.

How you perform after your review is equally important. If you receive a positive performance review, don't get lazy. Be sure to continue to do the things that helped you get that good review. Find out if there is anything else you can do to further improve your performance. If you get a bad review, make sure you understand how you can improve your performance, and then do everything you can to become a more satisfactory employee.

Unfortunately, employees sometimes receive unfair reviews. If you were surprised by a bad review, wait a couple of days before you do anything. A bad review might make you feel so upset that you can't think straight. That's not the time to have a conversation with your boss. After you've calmed down, think about the feedback that you received. If you disagree with anything that your employer said, make a list of examples that show that you did not deserve the negative feedback. If you have it, show your employer proof that you did your job correctly. For example, if your employer says that you have poor communication skills, show him or her emails that show that you communicate well with your team members.

Remember that a performance evaluation is an opportunity for you to communicate with your boss about his or her expectations and to learn if you are meeting those expectations. If you prepare for the review and use the information to help you improve, you will find that it can be a positive experience.

Writing: Creating a Job Advertisement

A Read the job descriptions. Check (✓) the categories below that each advertisement includes. Then underline the information for each category in the advertisements.

Job 1	Job 2
☐ Job Title	☐ Job Title
☐ Skills	☐ Skills
☐ Education/Experience	☐ Education/Experience
☐ Tasks	☐ Tasks
☐ Hours/Days	☐ Hours/Days
☐ Contact Information	☐ Contact Information
☐ Salary	☐ Salary
☐ Benefits	☐ Benefits

Job 1

ADMINISTRATIVE ASSISTANT

Medical and dental benefits

County Hospital seeks a detail-oriented person with good oral and written communication skills to join their team in San Francisco.

Duties include word processing, writing reports, answering phones, and assisting with various administrative functions. Requires 2 years experience performing related secretarial duties, typing. Candidates must be proficient in Microsoft Word & Excel.

Submit resume to County Hospital Human Resources, fax (415) 555-8879 or resumes@MMCCountyHospital.org.

Job 2

Looking for Certified Electricians

Candidates must have at least 2 years experience. Must have your own tools, and be reliable and punctual. Must also have valid driver's license.

Salary depends on experience.

Candidates must provide proof of Electrician's Certification. Must apply in person.

You may reach us @ 619-555-9500. Office address: 44673 Marcus Blvd, San Diego, CA by appointment only M-F 8-3

Hours are flexible.

B Write a job description for the job outlined below.

Job Title: _Restaurant Manager_

Skills: _math skills, interpersonal skills, leadership skills_

Education/Experience: _High School Diploma, 5 years management experience_

Tasks: _manage 12 employees, customer service, balance register_

Hours/Days: _Sun to Thur 1:30 to 10:30 PM, Fri & Sat 2:30 to 11:30 pm_

Contact Information: _Meg@CafeMeg.com_

Salary/Benefits: _$12.00 an hour, paid vacation_

TAKE IT OUTSIDE: USING YOUR FAVORITE SEARCH ENGINE, TYPE "JOB LISTINGS." FIND A JOB ADVERTISEMENT THAT INCLUDES ALL OF THE CATEGORIES LISTED IN ACTIVITY A. WRITE THE INFORMATION BELOW.

Job Title: _____

Skills: _____

_____

Education/Experience: _____

Tasks: _____

_____

Hours/Days: _____

Contact Information: _____

Salary/Benefits: _____

Community: Career Quiz

A   Take a career quiz. Check the answers that are true for you.

1. I like to work
   - ☐   indoors
   - ☐   outdoors
   - ☐   both indoors and outdoors

2. I enjoy working
   - ☐   alone
   - ☐   with a few people
   - ☐   with a lot of people

3. My favorite subject in school is
   - ☐   math
   - ☐   science
   - ☐   English
   - ☐   physical education
   - ☐   history
   - ☐   home economics or cooking
   - ☐   art
   - ☐   other: _____

4. I want a career that requires
   - ☐   a high school diploma or a GED
   - ☐   a certificate
   - ☐   a Bachelor's Degree
   - ☐   a Master's Degree
   - ☐   none of the above

5. I would feel satisfied at the end of my work day if I
   - ☐   saved someone's life
   - ☐   helped people
   - ☐   wrote something
   - ☐   made something with my hands
   - ☐   taught something
   - ☐   repaired something
   - ☐   other: _____

6. I want to work
   - ☐   a regular 9-5 shift
   - ☐   in the evenings
   - ☐   in the mornings
   - ☐   any time

7. I want to work
   - ☐   part time
   - ☐   full time

8. I like to have
   - ☐   one large task at a time
   - ☐   several small tasks at a time
   - ☐   a combination of large and small tasks

B   Write a description of yourself. Use the information from the quiz.

EXAMPLE: I want to work indoors with a lot of people. My favorite subject in school was math. I want a career that requires a Bachelor's Degree, so I have to enroll in college.

_____

_____

_____

_____

_____

_____

C Make a list of three possible careers for you, based on your answers to the career quiz. Write one reason that you chose each possible career. Then choose the career that sounds most interesting.

1. career: _____

   reason: _____

2. career: _____

   reason: _____

3. career: _____

   reason: _____

My preferred career: _____

D Read about informational interviews. Then make a list of four places in your community where you can do informational interviews for the career that you chose in Activity B.

> **Informational interviews** are a good way to learn more about a career. In an informational interview, you go to a workplace and ask people about their career. Through informational interviews, you can also meet people who might help you get a job in the future.

1. _____

2. _____

3. _____

4. _____

E Write five questions that you would like to ask in an informational interview.

Place: _____

1. _____

2. _____

3. _____

4. _____

5. _____

Family: A Typical Day

A Study the pie chart and read the sentences below. Check (✓) *True* or *False*.

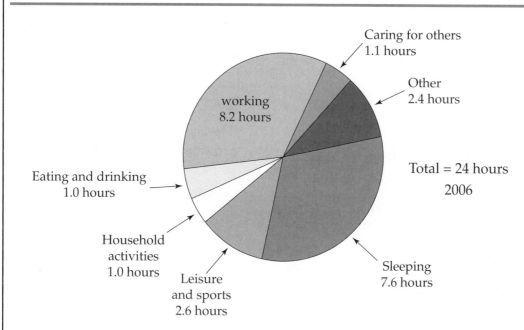

On weekdays that they worked, employed persons with children spent two-thirds of an average day working and sleeping

Caring for others
1.1 hours

Other
2.4 hours

working
8.2 hours

Total = 24 hours
2006

Eating and drinking
1.0 hours

Household
activities
1.0 hours

Leisure
and sports
2.6 hours

Sleeping
7.6 hours

NOTE: Data are for weekdays (Monday-Friday) only and refer to employed persons ages 25 to 54 who worked on the diary day and lived in households with children under 18. All categories, except sleeping and working, include related travel time. Data are 2006 annual averages.

SOURCE: Bureau of Labor Statistics

	True	False
1. According to the chart, working people with children sleep over eight hours a day.	☐	☐
2. Working people with children spend more than one third of the workday working.	☐	☐
3. The smallest percentage of the day is spent caring for others.	☐	☐
4. Working people with children spend a little over an hour eating and drinking.	☐	☐
5. People who work and have children spend less than two and a half hours doing fun things.	☐	☐
6. Ten percent of the day is spent doing "other" things.	☐	☐

B List the different activities you do during a typical day. If you have a job, list the activities that you do on a workday. Write the amount of time you spend on each activity. Make sure that the time adds up to 24 hours.

Activity	Time

C Make a pie chart that shows how you spend your time on a typical workday.

D Complete the chart below. Compare your pie chart with the pie chart in Activity A. Do you spend more or less time doing each activity than the average person does?

	More time than average	Less time than average
1. working		
2. caring for others		
3. eating and drinking		
4. leisure and sports		
5. household activities		
6. sleeping		
7. other		

Practice Test

DIRECTIONS: Read the work schedule below to answer the next 6 questions. Use the Answer Sheet.

Day	Morning Shift	Afternoon Shift	Evening Shift
Monday **July 1**	Paul ~~George~~ John (hw)	Tammy ~~John~~ George (hw)	~~Ruby~~ Eva (hw) Ken
Tuesday **July 2**	Alex John	Paul ~~Marta~~ Ken (hw)	Ruby ~~Ken~~ Marta (hw)
Wednesday **July 3**	~~Ruby~~ Eva (hw) Marta	Tammy George	Luis Ken
Thursday **July 4**	Closed for Independence Day		
Friday **July 5**	~~Eva~~ Tammy (hw) John	~~Tammy~~ Eva (hw) George	~~Carrie~~ Tomas (hw) ~~Ruby~~ Ken
Saturday **July 6**	~~Ruby~~ Luis (hw) John	~~Paul~~ Alex (hw) Marta	Carrie Paul

1. _____ has the day off on Wednesday.
   A. Tammy
   B. Eva
   C. Paul
   D. Luis

2. _____ is going to switch shifts with _____ on Friday.
   A. Carrie / Tomas
   B. Tammy / Eva
   C. Ken / Ruby
   D. George / John

3. _____ is going to work for _____ on Monday.
   A. Ruby / Eva
   B. Eva / Ruby
   C. Tammy / John
   D. Paul / John

4. The business is closed for a holiday on _____.
   A. Wednesday
   B. Thursday
   C. Friday
   D. Saturday

5. Marta has the day off on _____.
   A. Tuesday
   B. Wednesday
   C. Friday
   D. Saturday

6. Eva _____ on Wednesday.
   A. is switching shifts with Ruby
   B. is working for Ruby
   C. has the day off
   D. is going to leave early

ANSWER SHEET

	A	B	C	D
1	Ⓐ	Ⓑ	Ⓒ	Ⓓ
2	Ⓐ	Ⓑ	Ⓒ	Ⓓ
3	Ⓐ	Ⓑ	Ⓒ	Ⓓ
4	Ⓐ	Ⓑ	Ⓒ	Ⓓ
5	Ⓐ	Ⓑ	Ⓒ	Ⓓ
6	Ⓐ	Ⓑ	Ⓒ	Ⓓ
7	Ⓐ	Ⓑ	Ⓒ	Ⓓ
8	Ⓐ	Ⓑ	Ⓒ	Ⓓ
9	Ⓐ	Ⓑ	Ⓒ	Ⓓ
10	Ⓐ	Ⓑ	Ⓒ	Ⓓ

B Use the information below to answer the next 4 questions. Use the Answer Sheet on page 164.

Employee Performance Evaluation

EMPLOYEE	TITLE
Lisa Lee	Administrative Assistant

1 = Excellent   **2** = Very Good   **3** = Satisfactory   **4** = Decreased Performance   **5** = Unsatisfactory

Job Responsibilities	Rating	Comments
PUNCTUALITY The employee is on time and follows the rules for breaks.	5	Ms. Lee is sometimes 15 to 20 minutes late.
BEHAVIOR The employee is polite on the job.	1	Ms. Lee is very polite to clients and coworkers.
RELIABILITY The employee can be relied on to efficiently complete a job.	1	Ms. Lee always finishes her work before she goes home for the day.
INITIATIVE The employee looks for new tasks and expands abilities professionally.	1	Ms. Lee often asks for extra assignments because she finishes her work early. She is taking a management class and hopes to be promoted to office manager.
INTERPERSONAL SKILLS The communicates, cooperates, and works well with coworkers, supervisors, and customers.	4	Ms. Lee does not always tell her coworkers and supervisor what she is working on. She often does not participate in decision making.

7. Ms. Lee needs to improve her _____.

   A. punctuality
   B. behavior
   C. initiative
   D. reliability

8. One of Ms. Lee's strengths is her _____.

   A. creativity
   B. ability to make decisions
   C. communication
   D. ability to get her work done

9. One day, Ms. Lee hopes to be _____.

   A. a supervisor
   B. an office manager
   C. an administrative assistant
   D. a client

10. Ms. Lee needs to become a better _____.

   A. manager
   B. team leader
   C. communicator
   D. writer

HOW DID YOU DO? Count the number of correct answers on your answer sheet. Record this number in the bar graph on the inside back cover.

Comparing International Celebrations

A   Complete each sentence with a word from the box.

actually	celebrate	honor
ancestors	customary	legend

1. It's _____ to bring a small gift when you go to someone's house for dinner.

2. I thought Thanksgiving was on the first Thursday of November, but _____ it's on the last Thursday.

3. According to _____ , tea was first discovered in China when some leaves fell into a pot of boiling water.

4. My family meets once a year to _____ my grandfather. He was a very important part of our family.

5. Sue's birthday is on Tuesday, but she's going to _____ on Friday.

6. My _____ first arrived in this town two hundred years ago.

B   Write the name of the correct celebration under each picture. Then write a sentence on a separate piece of paper describing what is happening in the picture.

Cinco de Mayo	St. Patrick's Day	Mid-Autumn Festival	Carnival

①   Celebration: _____

②   Celebration: _____

③   Celebration: _____

④   Celebration: _____

C List your three favorite celebrations. Then describe what you do to celebrate.

Celebration	What do you do?
1.	
2.	
3.	

D Combine each pair of sentences to make a sentence with an adjective clause as the subject. Use *that* or *who*.

1. We went to a parade. The parade included a marching band.

   _____

2. We ate some corn. The corn was cooked on sticks.

   _____

3. We have some national holidays. These holidays commemorate historical figures like George Washington.

   _____

4. My best friend is a woman. She makes costumes and masks for parties.

   _____

5. The soccer players are celebrating St. Patrick's Day. They are wearing green shoes.

   _____

6. When I travel, I like to experience the customs. These customs are part of the new culture.

   _____

7. One celebration is the Mid-Autumn Festival. The celebration is popular in China.

   _____

Discussing Work and Family Balance around the World

A Look at the two charts. Read each statement and check *True* or *False*.

Country	Paid maternity leave (in weeks)	Percentage of salary paid	Unpaid maternity leave (in weeks)
China	12	100%	0
France	16	100	104 (shared with father)
Great Britain	39	90 for 6 weeks	26
Japan	14	N/A	0
Mexico	12	N/A	0
United States	0	N/A	12

Country	Paid paternity leave (in weeks)	Percentage of salary paid	Unpaid paternity leave (in weeks)
China	0	N/A	0
France	2	100	104 (shared with mother)
Great Britain	2	90 or a maximum of £123.06	0
Japan	0	60	0
Mexico	0	100	0
United States	0	N/A	12

	True	False
1. Women in China get more weeks of paid maternity leave than women in Mexico.	☐	☐
2. Women in Great Britain get the most paid maternity leave.	☐	☐
3. Women in the United States are guaranteed 12 weeks of paid maternity leave.	☐	☐
4. Women in France are guaranteed 12 weeks of paid maternity leave.	☐	☐
5. Women in Great Britain get the most unpaid maternity leave.	☐	☐
6. Men in Great Britain get 100% of their salary for two weeks of paid paternity leave.	☐	☐
7. Both men and women in France get 100% of their salary during their paid maternity/paternity leave.	☐	☐
8. Men and women in China get the same amount of paid and unpaid maternity/paternity leave.	☐	☐

B Complete each sentence with a word from the box.

average	conclude	mandatory	statistics
balance	households	service	wage earner

1. Based on the chart, we can _____ that paternity leave is very important to the French.

2. It's easy to work too much and not have time for family, so it's important to find a healthy _____ between the two parts of your life.

3. My wife is the main _____ in our home. She has a full-time job. I work only two days a week.

4. Some _____ show that workers in Mexico and China work 20% more hours per week than work- ers in the United States.

5. The _____ worker in the United States works 40 hours per week.

6. Many people feel that everyone should have paid maternity and paternity leave. They write letters to the government asking for _____ leave for new parents.

7. A large percentage of _____ in the United States have two wage earners.

8. After one year of _____ at my company, I'll get two weeks of vacation. After I've worked there for five years, I'll get three weeks of vacation.

C Answer the questions below.

1. How many hours a week do you spend at work? _____

2. How many hours a week do you spend at school? _____

3. How many hours a week do you spend with your family and friends? _____

4. Do you feel you have a good balance between work and your family and friends? Why or why not?

_____

_____

_____

_____

5. What are two things you can do to improve your work/family balance?

_____

_____

_____

_____

Understanding Cultural Behavior

A Read the advice column. Then write a response to each letter. Tell the writer what he or she did wrong and what he or she should do in that situation.

Dear Ms. Etiquette,

A coworker invited me over to her home for dinner last week. I was nervous about going to a party where I didn't really know anyone, so I brought a friend with me. When we arrived, I gave the host some flowers and introduced her to my friend.

During dinner, we found out that we both enjoy playing golf. I told her that I don't play often because it's expensive. She said that she didn't care about the cost because she loved golf. I asked her what her salary was, but she didn't tell me.

The dinner was delicious and I complimented my host at the end of the party. She was friendly, but I felt that I had done something wrong. What did I do?

Confused in California

Dear Confused,

_____
_____
_____
_____
_____
_____
_____
_____
_____
_____
_____

Ms. Etiquette

DearMs. Etiquette,

I had dinner at a new friend's house last week and now she seems to be uncomfortable around me.

When I arrived at her house, I had a book with me. I saw her looking at my book, so I told her about it. I bought it at my church. I asked her to come to church with me sometime because I thought she'd enjoy it.

Later, we talked about our favorite movies. Then I noticed that she was reading a book about American politics. I told her who I voted for in the last election, but she didn't tell me who she voted for.

I've called her three times since the dinner party, and she hasn't returned my calls. Did I do something wrong?

Baffled in Buffalo

Dear Baffled,

_____
_____
_____
_____
_____
_____
_____
_____
_____
_____

Ms. Etiquette

B Unscramble the questions. Then write an answer to each question.

1. okay / is it / at a dinner party / doesn't eat / something that he doesn't like / if someone?

_____?

Answer: _____

2. brings a beverage / at a friend's house / all right / if someone / is it / to a dinner party

_____?

Answer: _____

3. before the host / is it / to start eating / begins eating / appropriate /

_____?

Answer: _____

4. brings an expensive gift / if someone / is it / to a dinner party / all right

_____?

Answer: _____

C Combine each pair of sentences to make a sentence using an adjective clause with an object pronoun. Use *who* or *that*.

1. I brought my friend a box of chocolates. I bought the chocolates on my vacation.

_____

2. I invited some people to my party. I met the people last week.

_____

3. The flowers were beautiful. Ana gave me the flowers.

_____

4. Ana always brings me flowers. She grows the flowers in her garden.

_____

5. The parties are great. Mike and Cara host the parties.

_____

6. Cara baked a cake. Her grandmother taught her how to bake the cake.

_____

7. The dinner party lasted too long. I went to the dinner party on Friday night.

_____

Recognizing Bias and Stereotyping

A Read the short conversation under each photo. The speakers are using stereotypes. Below each photo, write the assumption that the speakers are making and the reason they're making the assumption.

1

A: Let's ask Tim to play on our football team.

B: Yeah, he's probably a great player.

Assumption: _____

_____

Reason: _____

_____

2

A: Did you ask Beth to join our book club?

B: I don't think Beth has time for book clubs. She probably has a date every night.

Assumption: _____

_____

Reason: _____

_____

3

A: I heard you're looking for a babysitter. My son is available.

B: Oh, well, uh, that's OK. I think I'm going to ask Jack's daughter.

Assumption: _____

_____

Reason: _____

_____

4

A: I went hiking with my Aunt Rita last weekend.

B: Really? Wow, I'm surprised.

Assumption: _____

_____

Reason: _____

_____

B Have you ever been guilty of stereotyping? Think of an occasion when you made an unconscious assumption about someone. What did you assume? Why? How did your assumption affect your behavior toward that person? Write a paragraph describing the situation.

_____

_____
_____
_____
_____
_____
_____
_____
_____
_____
_____
_____
_____
_____
_____
_____

C Complete the sentences. Use _you_, _one_, _we_, or _some_ and the correct form of the verb in parentheses.

1. _____We shouldn't judge_____ (should / judge / not) people based on the way they look.

2. Most people try not to stereotype, but (be / not) _____ aware that stereotyping is hurtful.

3. _____ (assume / not) anything about a person _____ (know / not).

4. When _____ (make) unconscious assumptions about people, _____ (be) often wrong.

5. I think that _____ (should / say) something when _____ (see) a person stereotyping someone else.

6. _____ (can / find) evidence of stereotyping in the media very easily.

7. _____ (might / think) stereotyping now and then is OK, but if _____ (do) regularly, it becomes a bad habit.

8. When _____ (assume) that someone can do something based on the way they look, that's stereotyping.

Reading: Comparing and Contrasting

A Read the passage. Highlight or underline words and phrases that describe the different cultures. Write them in the chart.

Visiting or moving to another country can cause a certain amount of culture shock for anyone. The extent of your culture shock depends on how different your own culture is from the new culture.

Mexico and the United States have some similarities. One thing that the people of Mexico and the people of the United States have in common is pride in their countries. There are also some similarities in the federal governments of the two countries. For example, like the United States, Mexico's government is divided into three branches: executive, legislative, and judicial.

Although Mexico and the United States share a border and a few similarities, it's easy to find cultural differences between the two countries. In Mexican culture, for example, family is more important than work. In the U.S., however, people often put work before family. Also, religion plays a big role in Mexican culture. Although religion is important to many Americans, religious beliefs are more diverse in the U.S. and therefore, religion isn't as visible in the U.S. as it is in Mexico.

There are a few differences when it comes to work, as well. At work, dress and appearance are status symbols in Mexican culture. It's important to look professional and put together. In contrast, Americans do not always prioritize dress and appearance in the same way. Although most Americans do try to look their best at work, it is not unusual to see someone dressed in jeans and a t-shirt in an office in the U.S. In a workplace in Mexico, you might find that coworkers are quite formal and polite with each other. In the United Sates, however, coworkers may be very informal with each other. American coworkers may also be more likely to confront each other or openly disagree with each other than Mexican coworkers.

Mexican Culture	American Culture

B Complete the Venn Diagram with the information from Activity A.

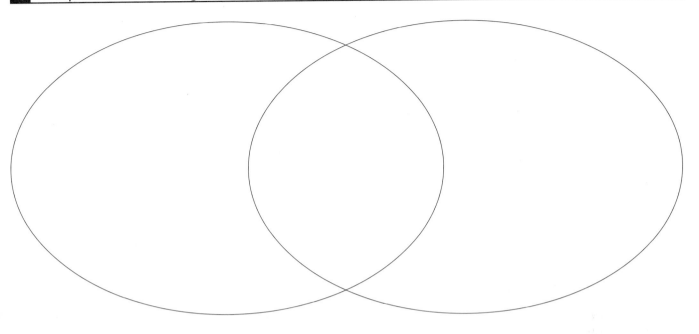

C Change each active sentence to make it passive. When the subject of the active sentence is *someone*, do not include *by* + noun.

1. Someone will ask the new students to arrive early.

_____

2. An administrator will give you directions.

_____

3. Someone will provide lunch for the students.

_____

4. Someone will explain the cultural differences to you.

_____

5. Ms. Bennett will interview Mario on Thursday.

_____

6. Someone will require you to fill out a form.

_____

7. The administration office will send out the grades next week.

_____

Writing: Communicating by Email

A Read each statement and check *True* or *False*.

		True	False
1.	You should always type something in the subject line of a business email.	☐	☐
2.	Use all capital letters to indicate that your email is important.	☐	☐
3.	Don't use abbreviations such as JK (just kidding) in business emails.	☐	☐
4.	You should respond to a business email within two hours.	☐	☐
5.	Don't discuss confidential information in a business email.	☐	☐
6.	If someone asks a lot of questions in an email, you should call them rather than send them an email back.	☐	☐
7.	If you use your email account for business, you should include your full name in the email address.	☐	☐

B Read the email. Circle four things that the writer did wrong.

☐ ＋ ☒

From: footballfan@speedymail.com

Subject: changing shifts

Date: March 14, 2010
To: lilywong44@speedymail.com

Hi Lily,

Thanks for your email. I'm so sorry it took me three days to get back to you.

I understand that you want to change from the evening shift to the morning shift, but I have a few questions.

First, do you go to school? And if so, what is your school schedule? Also, I need to know whether you can use a computer. Can you use Microsoft Word? How about Excel?

I was also wondering if you have a driver's license. Sometimes, employees on the morning shift have to make deliveries. Do you have your own car?

Regarding your question about salary, yes, I can give you a 5% raise. But please don't tell anyone. You will be making more money than anyone else after you get your raise.

Let's talk soon,

Max

C Write answers to the questions in the email in Activity B. Use your imagination.

1. _____
2. _____
3. _____
4. _____
5. _____

D Use your answers in activity C to write a reply to Max.

From: lilywong44@speedymail.com

Subject: Re: changing shifts

Date: March 15, 2010
To: footballfan@speedymail.com

Dear Max,

_____
_____
_____
_____
_____
_____
_____
_____
_____
_____
_____
_____

Work: Cultural Differences

A Read the article and answer the questions on page 179.

Cultural Differences in the Workplace

During your career, you may find yourself with the opportunity to work with a person from a country that you are unfamiliar with. When this happens, it can be helpful to make yourself familiar with the business customs of that country. If you don't, you could make an embarrassing mistake or misunderstand someone's behavior.

Greetings might be your first experience with another country's business culture. In the United States, greetings are often short and quick. In Cameroon, however, it is important not to rush greetings. When people in Cameroon greet each other, they ask each other about their families, their health, and other non-business related topics. And in South Korea, people greet each other with a bow, often followed by a handshake. The person who has lower status begins the bow, but the person with higher status begins the handshake.

In the United States, people are expected to arrive at the scheduled time for business meetings. Similarly, people are expected to arrive on time or a few minutes early for business meetings in China. In contrast, in some Brazilian cities, such as Rio de Janeiro, it is acceptable to be a few minutes late. So if a person from Rio is late for a business meeting, don't assume that the person meant to be rude or inconsiderate.

If you are invited to dinner at a German person's home, it's important to arrive on time. You may bring your host a small gift, such as chocolate or flowers. But if you are invited to an Argentinean home for dinner, you will probably be expected to arrive 30 to 45 minutes late. Again, it is common to bring a small gift for your host.

In the United States, hosts expect their guests to accept food the first time it is offered. If a guest refuses, the host will probably assume that the guest simply doesn't want the food or doesn't like it. However, In India, dinner guests are expected to politely refuse snacks or drinks the first time they are offered. Guests then are expected to accept the snacks or drinks the second time they are offered. The same is true in Bolivia.

If someone from another culture behaves differently than you expect, don't be offended. It may just be that their customs are different from yours.

QUESTIONS

1. How do people in Cameroon greet each other?

   _____

2. How do people in South Korea greet each other?

   _____

3. When are people expected to arrive for business meetings in China?

   _____

4. When should you arrive for a dinner party at an Argentinean home?

   _____

5. What should you do if you are offered tea in an Indian home?

   _____

6. Why is it important to understand the customs of different cultures?

   _____

C Answer the questions about your home culture. Write complete sentences.

1. How do people greet each other?

   _____

   _____

2. When are people expected to arrive at business meetings?

   _____

3. What are guests expected to do when they are offered a snack or a drink?

   _____

   _____

4. Have you ever been confused by a difference between your culture and another culture? Explain.

   _____

   _____

   _____

   _____

Family: Family Cultures

A Read the article and answer the questions below.

You know that each country has its own culture. But did you know that families have their own cultures, too? Every family is different. They come in different sizes. Some have children and some don't. Some include grandparents while others include friends. Even a group of roommates might have a kind of family culture. And like every country has its customs, every family has its own ways of doing things.

For example, Family A might have a rule about dinnertime. Perhaps everyone is expected to be at the dinner table at 6:00 P.M. Also, the children in that family might have jobs to do at dinnertime, such as helping cook and cleaning up after dinner. On the other hand, all of the members of Family B might be expected to make their own dinners.

Families have different routines as well. On a typical weekend, Family A might do weekly chores. The children may have to clean their rooms or mow the lawn. The parents may do the grocery shopping or make repairs around the house. Family B's weekend routine might include fun activities like going to a baseball game or to a museum.

Families also have different goals. Family A's goal might be to send all the children to college. Family B's goal might be to encourage each child to do what he or she wants to do after high school. The roles in different families may vary as well. For example, in Family A, the mother might be the main wage-earner. In Family B, there might be only one wage-earner. Or Family B might be a two-income household.

Whatever your family culture is like, it's important to understand your family's rules, routines, goals, and roles, and to respect those in other people's families.

Answer the questions about your family. If you live alone, describe your family when you were growing up. Or if you have roommates, you can describe that situation.

1. What is one of your family's rules?

   _____

   _____

2. Describe one of your family's routines.

   _____

   _____

3. What is one of your family's goals?

   _____

   _____

4. What is your role in your family?

   _____

   _____

B Look at the photos of the families below. Under each photo, write one way in which your family is similar to this family, and one way in which your family is different.

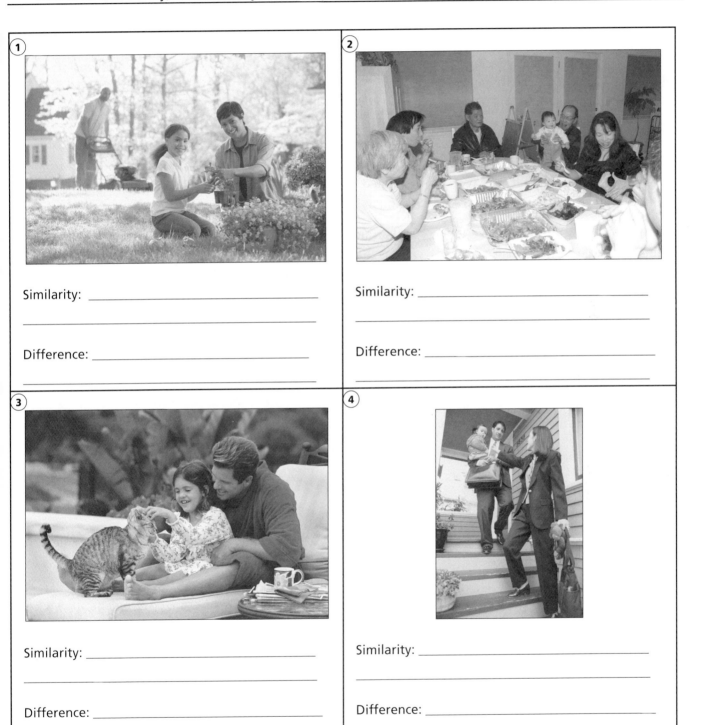

1

Similarity: _____

_____

Difference: _____

_____

2

Similarity: _____

_____

Difference: _____

_____

3

Similarity: _____

_____

Difference: _____

_____

4

Similarity: _____

_____

Difference: _____

_____

Practice Test

DIRECTIONS: Read the information below to answer the next 6 questions. Use the Answer Sheet.

Every year on July 14, the French celebrate their Independence Day. They call the holiday Bastille Day because it commemorates the liberation of the Bastille prison on July 14, 1789. At the time, France was ruled by King Louis XVI (the sixteenth) and Marie Antoinette. Many French citizens were poor and starving while the king and queen and a small percentage of upper-class citizens were wealthy and well-fed. The poor citizens were angry because they felt that they were being treated unfairly. They wanted a government that was fair and that paid attention to their needs.

In July of 1789, the citizens were angry and afraid. They attacked the Bastille and stole all the guns and other weapons that were kept in the prison. Then they freed the prisoners who were inside the prison. This event was the beginning of the French Revolution. At the end of the Revolution, France had a new kind of government without a king and queen.

Today, Bastille Day is celebrated in France with fireworks, parades, and parties. There are also formal Bastille Day celebrations in cities around the world, such as London, England, Budapest, Hungary, and New Orleans, Louisiana.

ANSWER SHEET

	A	B	C	D
1	Ⓐ	Ⓑ	Ⓒ	Ⓓ
2	Ⓐ	Ⓑ	Ⓒ	Ⓓ
3	Ⓐ	Ⓑ	Ⓒ	Ⓓ
4	Ⓐ	Ⓑ	Ⓒ	Ⓓ
5	Ⓐ	Ⓑ	Ⓒ	Ⓓ
6	Ⓐ	Ⓑ	Ⓒ	Ⓓ
7	Ⓐ	Ⓑ	Ⓒ	Ⓓ
8	Ⓐ	Ⓑ	Ⓒ	Ⓓ
9	Ⓐ	Ⓑ	Ⓒ	Ⓓ
10	Ⓐ	Ⓑ	Ⓒ	Ⓓ

1. Bastille Day is celebrated to commemorate _____.
   A. the opening of a prison
   B. the beginning of the French Revolution
   C. King Louis the XIV
   D. Marie Antoinette

2. Bastille Day is _____.
   A. July 14, 1789
   B. the 14th of June
   C. the same day as American Independence Day
   D. July 14th of every year

3. According to the reading, French citizens attacked the Bastille because _____.
   A. they wanted to free the prisoners
   B. they wanted to attack the King
   C. they were angry and afraid
   D. all of the above

4. When the citizens attacked the Bastille, they _____.
   A. freed prisoners and stole weapons
   B. freed prisoners and had a parade
   C. stole weapons and celebrated with fireworks
   D. celebrated with fireworks and parades

5. After the Revolution, _____.
   A. France had a different government
   B. France had a new king
   C. France elected a president
   D. King Louis began listening to the citizens

6. According to the reading, Bastille Day is celebrated _____.
   A. only in France
   B. in several global cities
   C. only in France and the United States
   D. in dozens of cities across Europe

B Use the information below to answer the next 4 questions. Use the Answer Sheet on page 182.

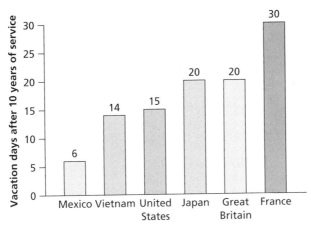

According to some statistics, workers in the United States have half as many paid vacation days after 10 years of service as French workers do. Workers in Mexico have one-fifth as much paid vacation as French workers do. Based on this information, you might conclude that the French have a better balance between work life and home life.

7. Workers in _____ have a little over twice as much vacation time as workers in Mexico.

   A. The United States

   B. Vietnam

   C. France

   D. Great Britain

8. Workers in Great Britain have the same amount of vacation time as workers in _____.

   A. Japan

   B. Vietnam

   C. France

   D. Great Britain

9. Workers in the United States get _____ less vacation than workers in Japan.

   A. 50%

   B. 25%

   C. 10%

   D. 75%

10. Workers in France have five times as many vacation days as workers in _____.

   A. Mexico

   B. Vietnam

   C. Japan

   D. the United States

HOW DID YOU DO? Count the number of correct answers on your answer sheet. Record this number in the bar graph on the inside back cover.

UNIT 2, PAGE 28
Lesson 4
Activity A, Answer Key

Workers' Health and Safety Quiz

1. Workers in the United States do NOT have the right to remove uncomfortable safety equipment.

2. Sprains and strains, usually involving the back, are the most common workplace injury.

3. False. Your boss cannot fire you for refusing to do unsafe work.

4. The construction industry has the most workplace fatalities.

5. False. Office workers DO have to worry about getting injured at work. Jobs that require repetitive motion such as typing or scanning groceries can cause serious injury to the hands and arms.

Correlation Table

Student Book Pages	Workbook Pages
PRE-UNIT	
2–3	2–3
UNIT 1	
4–5	4–5
6–7	6–7
8–9	8–9
10–11	10–11, 16–19
12–13	12–13
14–15	14–15
16–17	20–21
UNIT 2	
18–19	22–23
20–21	24–25
22–23	26–27
24–25	28–29, 34–37
26–27	30–31
28–29	32–33
30–31	38–39
UNIT 3	
32–33	40–41
34–35	42–43
36–37	44–45
38–39	46–47, 52–55
40–41	48–49
42–43	50–51
44–45	56–57

Student Book Pages	Workbook Pages
UNIT 4	
46–47	58–59
48–49	60–61
50–51	62–63
52–53	64–65, 70–73
54–55	66–67
56–57	68–69
58–59	74–75
UNIT 5	
60–61	76–77
62–63	78–79
64–65	80–81
66–67	82–83, 88–91
68–69	84–85
70–71	86–87
72–73	92–93
UNIT 6	
74–75	94–95
76–77	96–97
78–79	98–99
80–81	100–101, 106–109
82–83	102–103
84–85	104–105
86–87	110–111

Student Book Pages	Workbook Pages	Student Book Pages	Workbook Pages
UNIT 7		**UNIT 9**	
88–89	112–113	116–117	148–149
90–91	114–115	118–119	150–151
92–93	116–117	120–121	152–153
94–95	118–119, 124–127	122–123	154–155, 160–163
96–97	120–121	124–125	156–157
98–99	122–123	126–127	158–159
100–101	128–129	128–129	164–165
UNIT 8		**UNIT 10**	
102–103	130–131	130–131	166–167
104–105	132–133	132–133	168–169
106–107	134–135	134–135	170–171
108–109	136–137, 142–145	136–137	172–173, 178–181
110–111	138–137	138–139	174–175
112–113	140–141	140–141	176–177
114–115	146–147	142–143	182–183

All multiple photos on page, credits read left to right on page or top to bottom in a column.

Page 4: Mel Curtis/Photodisc/Getty; **5:** Photodisc/Getty; **6:** BananaStock/Alamy; **8:** Comstock/Punchstock; **15:** Comstock/Alamy; ImageSource/Punchstock; **27:** Mikael Karlsson/Alamy; **31:** The McGraw-Hill Companies, Gary He; **32:** moodboard/Corbis; **35:** DigitalVision/Punchstock; **41:** Jupiterimages; **42:** Photodisc/Getty; **46:** BananaStock; **48:** Rubberball Productions; The McGraw-Hill Companies; RF/Corbis; **50:** Kent Knudson/Getty; **59:** Getty/foodcollection; **62:** Jack Star/Photolink/Getty; **64:** 2007 Getty Inc.; **70:** RF/Corbis; **72:** RF/Corbis; BananaStock/Jupiterimages; BananaStock/Jupiterimages; Jack Star/Getty; **77:** Photolink/Getty; **80:** Erica S. Leeds; **86:** Nancy R. Cohen/Getty; **88:** Frederico Gil; **94:** RF/Corbis; **96:** S. Meltzer/Photolink/Getty; Peter Grzeley/Getty; **98:** Buccina Studios/Getty; **99:** C. Sherburne/Photolink/Getty; **103:** Library of Congress Prints & Photographs Division (LC USZ 62-26759); **112:** Corbis; Alex Maloney/Corbis; BrandX/Punchstock; **113:** The McGraw-Hill Companies, Jill Braaten; **116:** Steve Cole/Getty; **121:** RF/Corbis; **130:** Stockbyte; The McGraw-Hill Companies, Bob Coyle; Jules Frazier/Getty; D. Hurst/Alamy; Stockbyte/Getty; **154:** Bananastock; RF/Corbis; Stockdisc/Punchstock; Stockdisc; DigitalVision/Getty; Bananastock/Picturequest; **157:** Bananastock/Picturequest; **172:** RF/Corbis; Amos Morgan/Getty; Rubberball Productions; Creatas/Picturequest; **181:** Jupiterimages/Comstock/Alamy; RF/Corbis; Keith Eng 2007; RF/Corbis; Ryan McVay/Getty.